READER BONUS!

Dear Reader,

As a thank you for your support, I would like to offer you a special reader bonus: The 40-Day Woosah Gratitude Journal.

The Journal typically retails for $14.95, but as a valued reader, you can access the PDF version for free. To claim your free download, click on the QR code.

Kids Woosah Journal   Adults Woosah Journal

With Gratitude,
Martha

READER BONUS!

Author Email: picwellnessllc@gmail.com
Author Website: www.picwellnessllc.com
Publisher Email: lynda@actiontakerspublishing.com
Publisher Website: www.actiontakerspublishing.com

ISBN # (paperback) 979-8-218-42967-6
ISBN # (Kindle) 979-8-218-42968-3

Published by Action Takers Publishing™

GLORY

CULT
SURVIVOR
—— TO ——
COURAGEOUS
WARRIOR

Table of Contents

TABLE OF CONTENTS

Foreword

I am a big fan of personal development and leadership; anyone who knows me knows that about me. I wrote a book called *Today Is the Day*, which is about turning simple disciplines into massive success. The *Today Is the Day* Philosophy is simply the mindset and action steps about simple behaviors that works for anyone. The magic truly lies in the thoughts you think every single day, the details that don't look like they matter, that do matter, and make all the difference. I've always said if somebody wrote a book and they took their whole life to learn that knowledge in that book, why wouldn't you just read that book to learn what they know? I have been fortunate to be the CEO and owner of many successful companies. So how did I get there? Well, I've had some help. When you get the opportunity to be around Successful CEOs and influential authors and speakers, their wisdom has a way of rubbing off on you.

I met Martha Kartaoui at a business conference where I gave a keynote speech. Something spiritual was happening in that room. At first introduction, we hit it off amazingly well because we both believe in divine connections, which led directly to the completion of the book you have before you. What I did not know at that time was that Martha would become like family. She is a woman who serves others before herself. A great woman of true integrity isn't easy to come by, so I treasure those relationships when they come into my circle.

In 2007, before my life became significant, before I became a best-selling author, and before I became the CEO of several multi-million-dollar companies, my life was up in flames, and I was homeless trying to survive. In her book, *Glory: Going All In*, Martha takes a deep dive into what she calls the principles, the core to her non-negotiables. I believe everyone who has experienced trauma should be doing these things daily to bulletproof their life. She calls it the **GOING ALL IN** Principles.

If I knew this acronym for building my first business during my own personal trauma journey, which was a struggle, my success would have catapulted much sooner. It is for this exact reason I highly recommend you read this book several times to master the practices. Great leaders don't just tell you what to do, they demonstrate through action consistently. I was not surprised to see an Email from her asking about writing the foreword to this amazing body of work. Naturally, I had to support and urge everyone to use this book as a building tool as soon as possible and most importantly make sure your friends and family who experienced trauma get a copy as well. Besides her accomplishments as an entrepreneur, getting to know the woman personally, Martha is an amazing Christian, she has a heart for worship and most importantly she enjoys helping others. This book certainly expresses that by highlighting how you can follow the same sequence into building your confidence and overcoming obstacles. Her stories are relatable, practical and relevant for today's ever-changing market.

Glory: Going All In is simply a book that mirrors the everchanging escape from cult life's journey through struggles, failures and triumphs. *Glory* shares the inner struggles we all face and delivers a powerful message through relatable modern and timeless stories. Regardless of your background, whether you are currently stuck, or suffered from stagnation, financial decline, and everything else in-between, Martha shares her stories and experiences and breaks down the gap between you having to suffer alone and you truly knowing you can come out on the other side stronger. My biggest takeaway is really understanding her ability to persevere to which you as the reader would be keen to in Chapter 4 "Time to Cleanse," the truth is, our acts can be no wiser than our thoughts. Our thinking can be no wiser than our understanding. If you intend to be successful in your process, Martha shares the strategies that she has proven to command the results you desire.

I was so happy, honored really, when I was asked by Martha to write the foreword for this book. Her combination of pure grit, personal development, practical steps and life stories are just so relatable to hard topics unknown to our generation. This book may well be destined to become your favorite inspirational read this year and many to come. Martha demonstrates in her book *Glory: Going All In*, her ability for awakening the sleeping spirit residing within every one of us that is most welcome in a time of change and challenge. This book is simply thought inspiring.

Be the Best,

Obom Bowen, Ph.D.
Founder and CEO, Underdog Millionaire **TM**
Author, Award Winning International Bestseller, *Today Is the Day*

Letter to the Reader

I write not only to tell my story, but rather to share hope, light and grace to all those who will read it. I want to share a short message with anyone who is reading this who has shared trauma experiences or any other painful experiences that you will read about in this book.

You are not your experiences! You are not your trauma! You are not your lowest points! You are not your shame, guilt, hopelessness, fear, anxiety or pain!

You are Worthy! You are love, hope, strength, and beauty! You are alive and, therefore, you have a responsibility to yourself to rise up, disrobe yourself of the burdens of your past, and breathe in the opportunities of release, healing, growth and love!

The trauma, pain, filth and vileness inflicted upon us is part of our story; it does not define us! We are so much more and you face the option in this moment to choose freedom and healing from your past and revel in the joy that your future has to offer or not. It's a choice. It's a process, often a painful one, but no pain can compare to the violence, betrayal and angst of our past, so choose healing, go all in, you are worth it!

In the following pages, you will read about my journey. Born into a religious cult, I witnessed and was plagued with physical, mental, emotional, spiritual, verbal and sexual abuse. I escaped from the compound during a divinely ordained winter blizzard in my mid-20s (you'll learn why and how in the book). I had to re-identify with who I was and who I wanted to be. It was a painstaking uncovering from all the labels, responsibilities, expectations and identities that were inflicted upon me in my first 25 years. When I awakened to the realization that I had the liberty to choose who I wanted to be in my future and was able to see who God had created me to be, well, that was exhilarating! And I decided to Go All In!

Now, I share in hopes of helping others with similar experiences to feel less alone, less abandoned, and less isolated in their pain. My prayer is that through my story others will see the potential within themselves to find their voice, purpose and own reason for choosing to heal. What will be your Going All In moment?

PART 1

Growing Up Culty

CHAPTER 1

Cultman

December 27, 2004, for me will always be a date that represents faith, courage, hope, strength, and resilience. That day is forever memorialized in my mind as the night that everything changed. I boldly and intentionally jumped faith first (not feet first) and took my life back. That was the night that I physically, spiritually and emotionally made my final escape from the clutches of the religious cult that I had been born into. Throughout the previous 25 years, my existence had been completely controlled and dictated by my family's involvement in this "group." I had been held enslaved in the leader's compound for almost eight years prior and it was nothing short of a living hell.

After 25 years, I finally decided, "Enough is enough. I refuse to live this way. I know this isn't right. This can't be all there is to life!" The praying, plotting and planning for my final escape had begun about 10 days prior to my voluntary evacuation. I had attempted an escape in 2000 and failed miserably. As you might imagine, the repercussions were excruciatingly painful. But this time felt different. I heard that Smyrna, my youngest sister, was pregnant with her first child. When I received the news, I was ecstatic! During that conversation, I promised her I would find a way to safely be with her during her pregnancy. I wasn't going to let her go through this special time alone. Afterall, I was the older sister and she needed me! I didn't have any idea how I was going to manage this daunting feat. I felt the enormity of my situation in every fiber of my being, but the heaviness seemed to give me determination instead of scaring me!

I was not allowed communication with most of my siblings because I was still "involved" in the cult and they had separated themselves years prior, making them excommunicated. In addition, I was held captive in the leader's compound (who we now refer to as "Cultman" and will refer to as "Cultman" throughout this book) and that's why I needed to escape. My every move was monitored. The only time I left the compound was to go to work. I worked for one of the cult owned businesses; we made fresh, homemade fudge and sold knick knacks. We were open 7 days a week from 9am-9pm 365 days per year and I worked all of those hours without time off for vacation, sick leave, or enjoyment, oh, and with no pay.

Growing up, I didn't know our group was a cult. I thought we were part of a secret society. The idea that the outside world was scary, evil and dangerous was ingrained in us, but we were safe because we were "the chosen." Looking back, I knew from a very young age that the outside world would not understand my family or our group because everything about us was different by design. The women wore long skirts and button-down blouses, no makeup or jewelry, and we weren't allowed to cut our hair. The enforced hairstyle for the women was hair parted down the middle or side and all wrapped up tightly in a bun on the back of our heads. The men dressed modestly as well. No blue jeans, shorts or tee shirts. Rather, they wore blue, tan or black dickeys with solid color button down shirts. It wasn't just our physical appearance that set us apart from the outside world; there were so many other things!

I knew I was different, but I never felt proud to be different because it didn't feel affirmative or positive. Rather, as a child I felt like a walking billboard of "you don't fit in, you are weird, why do you look like that, why do you act like that?" When going out in public, I always wanted to shrink myself and be as small as possible so that no one would notice how different I was because, inevitably, that always led to stares, glares or questions that I wasn't allowed or able to answer. It is really hard to hide a billboard, so I always stuck out everywhere I went, but not in a healthy or good way, more like in a circus freak kind of way.

From about age seven, I learned that lying was easier than telling the truth. It was necessary so that the outside world would not get wind to what was really going on in our group. For example, if someone asked me why I wore skirts all the time, I would tell them it was because I was orthodox Jewish, or Mormon, because somewhere along the line I learned that women of those religions wore skirts and dressed modestly. If someone asked me why I didn't eat chocolate, I told them I was allergic instead of explaining to them that chocolate was actually on our list of things that were forbidden because they were "of the world" and we weren't allowed to partake.

I am getting way ahead of myself. Let's rewind and go back to where and when it all started.

To my recollection, nothing from my childhood was normal according to today's standards starting as far back as my birth. My mom recalls that she was in labor with me for about 24 hours, but nothing terribly painful happened until right before I made my entrance. That was February 9, 1979, and she received me at around 2:20am, her water breaking just minutes before she delivered me. I am sure that the day of my birth was a typical winter early morning in southern Minnesota except that nothing about it sounds typical or normal. My mother chose to have an all-natural home birth. She had delivered three children before me, but all were born in the hospital.

My mom explains that my dad was present for my birth and they were assisted by Lane, a nurse they knew from the cult. In anticipation of my birth, a large aluminum pot with a long wooden handle was halfway filled with water, covered and placed on the stove to boil. Inside that pot were two white shoe laces and a pair of metal scissors. The items were boiled in order to be sterilized. My mom remembers having a sense of peace during my birth even though it was the first she had experienced at home. She was assisted in the entire process by Lane who explained each step as it was happening and told my mom what she needed to do. Upon my arrival, they tied off the umbilical cord in two places using the shoe laces and then used the scissors to cut between the two tied off ends. Within 40 minutes of my birth, my mom explained that she was up and out of bed taking a shower. For several days I was known as baby girl Stecker; that was until I could be prayed over, anointed with oil and given a name by Cultman.

Cultman is a short in stature, medium framed, balding man of Indian descent who is currently estimated to be in his early 80s, but no one knows for sure. He always wears a button down crisply ironed white shirt and gray or black pressed slacks. He wears a tie to all meetings and if he was cooking or outside managing or overseeing the manual labor sites, he would throw on a pair of gray coveralls to cover up his uniform. He had a distinct smell, one of bad breath mixed with soap and a musk cologne. As the story goes, he came to the United States from India to go to Grad School in his early 20s as a nuclear engineering student. A few years later, he had a vision from God that said he was to be the leader of God's chosen people. He began in the early '70s preaching the Christian gospel and sharing his vision and quickly gained a following and so The Disciples of the Lord Jesus were born. By the time I was born, the group no longer really had a name. In the 25 years that I was part of the cult, we were just known as the Brethren and Cultman was our revered and God-like leader. God-like because we were taught that he was our intercessor. We confided all things in him, and then he would take them to God for us. Our relationship was with him, not with God. The leader himself took on many name changes during my time in the group. I am not sure why, but, looking back, I surmise that he was probably running from something or someone.

Cultman was extremely dynamic and charismatic and people readily flocked to him. My parents recall that the first time they went to a meeting they were captivated by Cultman's message, and felt like they had found what they had been searching for, someone to lead them. My parents were hippies and they shared that the 1970s was a time when tons of people just like them were searching for something with meaning and were desperate to find somewhere to belong, something to believe in bigger than themselves. That is why Cultman's early messages were so appealing. He proclaimed divine messages that resonated in the souls of the searching and lost, and miracles were a common occurrence in those early years.

Cultman was married and had two children of his own. But to his followers, he was more than our father. We propped him up on a proverbial pedestal and treated him like a God, submitting ourselves totally to him. He was feared and praised and no one did anything without his permission or blessing. No decisions were made independently of Cultman. None! What job to take, what to name your child, what school to attend, what to do with a sick child, what foods were allowed, what we wore, whether to buy a house or car and everything in between are all examples of how intertwined Cultman was in all of our lives.

I am #4 in the birth order of nine children in my family of five boys and four girls. I was born in Mankato, Minnesota. After my birth, my mom proceeded to give birth to the next three of my siblings at home as well, no meds, no proper prenatal or postnatal care, just a blind faith that God would watch over her and her babies. To limit our exposure to the outside world, home births were an expectation of the women in our group. This was the same reason we didn't seek medical care when we were injured or seriously sick. Instead, we sought advice and guidance from Cultman. All of my siblings and I were named by Cultman, except the two that were born before my parents joined the group in 1975.

Growing up with so many siblings was a blessing as we always had each other. We were purposely limited in our interactions with the outside world or classmates. No TV, radio, newspapers, sleepovers, birthday parties, and no celebration of holidays. In fact, those were not allowed in the cult as a whole. We did not celebrate birthdays, anniversaries or holidays. Those were considered distractions and things of the "world," and we were not allowed to partake. Dietary restrictions evolved as Cultman felt led. I remember for years it was no chocolate, coffee, pasta, pizza, pork, tea, candy, soda, alcohol, etc. Then the rules and rituals changed as Cultman received from his source, and then translated them into law and practice for us. The Don't and Can't list evolved slowly as Cultman sank his manipulative, conniving, ego-driven claws further into every miniscule part of our existence.

Our lives were extremely regimented and controlled by Cultman, but this didn't seem strange to me because it was all I ever knew. In our group, each family had their own home. Brethren commuted to the cult property each weekend from parts of Minnesota, Wisconsin and Michigan. This was every single weekend. There was never the option of saying, thinking or feeling, oh I think I will take the weekend off and just stay home and relax. That was never an option! It didn't matter if a family member was sick or working late, they were not acceptable excuses.

Most families, including ours, rushed to gather up their families after a busy week and drove four to five hours one way each Friday and then spent the weekend working, worshiping, and fellowshipping at the compound and then drove back drained and exhausted to their homes late Sunday night just in time to go to work on Monday. This was the norm and expectation for all of the families in our group. Every single weekend was spent on the sprawling 200 and some acres where the compound was the focal point. There was always work to be done. Cultman knew that idle hands are the devil's playground so Cultman kept us busy, unless we were being punished by being put into a barrel for hours or days, sticking our nose to a metal pole for endless hours, making us sit and pray on our knees in one place and then further punished if we moved, or any number of other grueling punishments that were doled out at his whim.

The compound was a very large fortress looking structure made up of very large steel beams, steel plates and wood. The compound always had the appearance that it was under construction. For years on end, blue tarps covered unfinished parts of the structure. It sat on an expansive 200+ acres. Some of the land was cleared and was farmed. Other acreage was used for apple orchards, and a several acre garden. Other parts of the land included storage buildings, a large pond, a burn pile, and quite a bit was wooded and unmanicured. The top of the compound was where Cultman and his family lived and that part somewhat resembled a typical one story ranch house. From the outside it looked like it had a few bedrooms, then some common space, a kitchen and a garage. I am not really certain what exactly was up there, because I was never permitted to see. Most Brethren were never allowed up there. Only specially chosen ones were allowed in the spaces where

Cultman and his family lived. The rest of us knew only the bottom portion of the compound which was very much an open floor plan and was quite expansive.

The bottom part of the compound was made up of two large kitchens, one for Cultman to cook his personal meals, and one where he would cook meals for the Brethren. There were a couple of worship or meeting spaces that could accommodate all members at the same time, which ranged from 200 to 300. Then there were separate open spaces for sleeping/eating for the men/boys and the women/girls. All of these spaces had concrete floors; some spaces had plywood covering the concrete. All spaces had open beams of steel or wood overhead which were sometimes covered with spray foam insulation. The walls were all unfinished. Some had plywood, some had sheetrock, but none of them were painted. There were no carpets, benches, pews, plush beds, etc. or even bathrooms. There were no windows and only one very large, thick, heavy wooden door that led from the inside to the outside. It was probably 10 feet tall, and 6-8 inches thick. Outside the gigantic door were lines and lines of the Brethren's and their children's shoes and boots. No one wore shoes into the compound except Cultman or a few of his chosen helpers. The bottom space where all of the Brethren spent their time did not have heat or air conditioning for many years, but eventually did get both. It was still pretty cold in the winter and hot in the summer.

All of the Brethren brought their own sleeping bags, blankets, pillows and food. When it was time to sleep, we all lined up like sardines one right next to the other in our respected family segregated area. When we were allowed to eat, which was usually once or twice a day, families sat huddled together and ate in silence. The sharing of fellow Brethren's food was forbidden. Sometimes Cultman would cook for all of us which was definitely a treat and highlight. He would cook in a 20-gallon cast iron pot and make curry or sometimes he used a huge grill to cook chicken, steak or fish and handed out long french bread loaves to make sandwiches. I know it sounds like Cultman was so generous and just cooked for us out of the goodness of his heart, but all of it came at a cost. Several of the Brethren's daughters whom Cultman had chosen would slave over preparation for hours before the cooking ever took place and then spend several hours cleaning once he was done. He would basically get all the glory, but do very little of the work. Even though he cooked, it was all paid for by the members. He never cooked alone; he always had help from certain girls that were worthy of being allowed to touch food.

The compound did not have bathrooms, or at least ones that we were allowed to use. The bathroom or showers within the compound were upstairs and only for Cultman and his family's use or the very select few that he allowed. Our bathroom/showers were about a quarter of a mile away from the compound at a fellow Brethren's house. There were two houses next to one another and they were owned by two brothers. Those houses were where all of us used the bathroom and showered, all 200 to 300 of us. We showered twice a day, and as you can imagine this was a very lengthy process when dealing with this many people.

The showering process was very segregated as well. The mothers showered together, the girls together, the fathers together, and the boys showered together. In the house where my family used the bathroom and showered there were three shower stalls and our showers were only allowed to be a few minutes long. Hot water was a luxury, and unless you were one of the first groups the water was inevitably cold because the water heater could never keep up. There was only one bathroom in the house so we would stand in the bathroom line for hours waiting for our turn. This was extremely hard and painful after sitting in a meeting for eight to 10 hours without a bathroom break, and then Cultman would release us and all 200 to 300 of us would go running to the two houses and then still have to wait because there was only one bathroom at each house. Many wouldn't make it and would wet and soil their clothes on the way or in the line. This was just normal. No one picked on each other if they saw it because the next time it could be you. Some chose to run to the forest or the tree line to urinate instead of standing in the long lines. Many members would try to dehydrate themselves starting on Friday so that they wouldn't have these types of issues.

There were many times when I took a bath towel and put it under my skirt and then sat on it and wet it to relieve myself because I just couldn't make it to the bathroom. I would then put it in a trash bag so it could be washed later. I can still remember the pain of having to go to the bathroom during meetings and knowing that there were still hours to go before I would be able to make a run for the bathroom line. There were times in the meetings when we just wet ourselves because we were too scared to raise our hand and ask Cultman if we could go. If you did get brave and raise your hand and interrupt Cultman's sermon, two things could happen: 1) Cultman could nod and say yes you could go, or 2) he could completely humiliate you and tell you to sit down. The latter was more common than the former.

Worship meetings in the compound made up the majority of our weekends. They would begin usually around 6 o'clock in the morning and go until midafternoon. And then start again around 6 o'clock in the evening and go until around 10 o'clock. There were exceptions to this type of lengthiness, but it was only if some manual labor needed to be done. We would worship and sing songs, some old hymnals and others (that were made up by Cultman) for hours independent of Cultman. Then he would come down and preach a sermon for a couple of those hours sprinkled with some more singing/worshiping. All meetings were segregated. Steel beams in the middle of the meeting room separated the males from the females, and women with small children or ones that were nursing sat on the outside of the meeting room where they could still hear the sermon but could not be seen by the rest of the Brethren. We all sat on our knees on the plywood covered floor for the entire meeting. This is extremely hard on your knees and painful even if that is the way you grew up. It's just plain hard on your joints. When Cultman wasn't down, we sat side saddle or cross-legged but as soon as Cultman came down everyone was on their knees. Also, when Cultman wasn't down was when we would run to the outside of the meeting room to where everyone slept and wet a towel or pee in a bottle to try to ensure that we would not have to go to the bathroom during the actual sermon.

Side note: the houses where we went to the bathroom and showered were locked during meeting times so there was no way to sneak over there if you had to go to the bathroom.

Manual labor around the sprawling compound property ranged from sweeping rain water or snow off the deck, to weeding and planting the gardens, cutting grass with scissors, digging ponds and foundations with shovels and wheelbarrows, taking care of animals, adding or fixing different parts of the compound, setting new beams, pouring cement, hauling brush to the burn pile a mile or so away, cleaning the downstairs of the compound, weeding the forest, replanting the forest, watering the apple orchards, cleaning the Caterpillar dozer with a toothbrush, and the list goes on endlessly.

Cultman would assign people to whichever assignment or project was going on for that weekend. If you weren't selected, you stayed in the compound and worshiped or, if you got lucky, slept. Many of the projects were extremely dangerous and many people were hurt over the years. Many of the projects in retrospect were menial and given to us to just keep us busy. Some examples of this meaningless manual labor is digging holes then filling them in, or moving stones or rocks or something and then moving them back, pulling weeds in the woods, etc. But we were glad to do it, and most of the time we did it with all of our hearts until we realized how truly ridiculous it was. Cultman also bought and stockpiled a lot of things like very large steel beams, osb plywood, cement, nails, tools, sheetrock, steel plates (that served as a roof for most of the compound), etc. They would arrive on semi-trailers and then we would spend all day and night unloading them and then walking them ungodly distances to storage buildings. All of this was done by hand. No cranes or forklifts were onsite. I have so many memories of holding a flood light while others were working on some project until the wee hours of the morning. Other times were spent participating in a project and just praying that Cultman would come out and let us stop and go to bed. We never stopped or started anything without Cultman's direction.

CHAPTER 2

Innocence Gone

I was a full-spirited, energetic kid. I was curious, had a huge imagination, and was always on the go. My mom says that I was crawling by five months old and walking by nine months. I had places to go and things to get into! Even though we were in the cult, my family moved to a small farm town in Grand Meadow, Minnesota, when I was 18 months old. I still have so many fond memories of the time on that farm. The cornfields made for the best hide 'n seek games! The trees were for climbing and building forts! The yard circling the small 1100-square-foot farmhouse that housed my family of 11 was open for our imagination! My siblings and I basically lived outside, unless it was raining or snowing because we didn't have a TV, radio, video games, or any other distraction so our time was spent creating our entertainment and fun outside. We did not have toys or bikes, as those things were forbidden as well, but everything was a toy to us! We all had huge, healthy imaginations! Laundry baskets were sleds, Tupperware served as blocks, drums, storage for worms, spiders, beetles and more. I don't remember wishing that we had the forbidden things because my siblings and I made the best of everything that surrounded us. Nothing was off limits. If we could imagine it, then we did it. We swam fully clothed in the ditches after a big summer rain, ate watermelon on top of the 500-gallon propane tank as fireworks were put off in town on the 4th of July. We sled on metal cookie sheets off the top of my dad's shop's metal roof after a blizzard that left the snow drifting to the top of the building. We dug mud holes behind my dad's shop and played in them.

When I was ten years old, four or five of us kids were out digging a huge mud hole after a big rain. We all had a shovel or garden tool and were working seamlessly together to create the biggest best mud hole we had ever made! Suddenly, I screamed in agony! Everyone froze. I had been struck in the head by my brother Tim (then age 3 or so) with a triangle shaped garden hoe. Adam, my older brother, seeing what had happened, picked me up, put his hand over the gaping wound and ran with me into my dad's shop followed by a gaggle of siblings screaming, "Daddy, Martha's hurt!" My dad took me from Adam, and as Adam removed his hand from my head a geyser of blood shot out and then dripped down soaking my yellow shirt. My dad took his shirt off and tied it around my head and picked me up and rushed me inside to my mom. Mom and dad took me to the bathroom and put me in the shower and once again as soon as the shirt was removed from my head the wound gushed with blood. I remember my mom staying calm, but putting her hand on the wound and praying out loud and then began giving instructions. My head was partly shaved around the wound and then my mom carefully closed the gash with butterfly bandages, gauze and tape. Most likely I should have had stitches, but the closest hospital was over 30 minutes away and in our group you did not go to the hospital unless you absolutely had to. But by the grace of God, my siblings and I were spared any broken bone or any illness that required hospitalization until after we were out of the cult.

My dad, Bill, owned a custom woodworking manufacturing business on the property. All of us kids grew up in that shop. We would help clean, play or just tinker around. The storage shelves served as endless hours of fun for us kids climbing and hiding or just sleeping. Dad spent all of his time in this shop. He was an inventor and his shop was his playground and happy place. If you wanted to see dad, you went to the shop. I can remember many nights staying up very late in the shop helping dad finish up an order or holding a light or just watching and asking questions. All of us kids did that at one point or another.

My mom, Cathy, always had a garden. She has a green thumb, and basically everything that she touches grows and flourishes. All of us kids helped my mom plant the huge garden each year, and the fruits of that labor were endless and delicious come strawberry and blueberry picking season! Picking and eating fresh berries is still a favorite of mine. We also planted tomatoes, carrots, peppers, zucchini, yellow squash, pumpkin, potatoes, corn, cucumber, watermelon, cantaloupe, and more! The gardens were plentiful and we ate fresh food year round as mom canned plenty for us to enjoy during the winter months.

I entered public school in first grade at age six. The cult didn't believe in kindergarten as it was thought to be a waste of time and all about play and we believed kids needed structure and discipline. I remember that first bus ride as I joined all my older siblings waiting at the top of our gravel driveway for the bus. Our small farm town school was K-12 in the same school building, so we all rode the same bus as well.

It was painfully apparent very quickly that I had very little interest in school and struggled with the structure, required learning, and teaching style of the public school system. To say it was a challenge is an understatement. Everything was just hard and I didn't know why.

My brain just didn't work like others. My teachers thought I was lazy, disorderly and disruptive. My mom received notes from my teachers routinely regarding my inability to listen, pay attention or regarding my behavioral issues because I couldn't sit still. At the beginning of third grade I was labeled "mentally retarded" by my teacher and I was sent to the classroom with seriously disabled and non-verbal students.

My mom was furious when she found out about my classroom change. She jerked me out of school and had me tested. She refused to believe the label that had been put on me. Results came back, and we found our answer. I was severely dyslexic and had some ADD tendencies, thus why I couldn't read and why math just didn't compute for me and why everything was difficult for me when it came to learning.

Mom found resources to help me and she proceeded to homeschool me for the next year and a half until I was back up to grade level and then I returned to public school. I have so much respect for my mom for making the choice to homeschool me during that time period because she had her hands full with three small children and all the cooking, cleaning and laundry for a family of 11, all while trying to teach and corral an ADD and dyslexic, rambunctious child. Many days I would sneak out to the shop when I was supposed to be studying and just hang out with dad and his workers.

There was this particular guy, Danny, who showed me special attention and made me feel good. He would give me compliments and give me small jobs to do and just seemed to really like having me around. One day he invited me to his parent's farm, which was about two miles from our house, to ride horses. I was so excited! I had never been on a horse before. My parents said I could go, and off on his moped we rode. We arrived at the farm and he did take me to see the horses, but he never let me ride them. That was the first time that he started touching me. Danny was 24 years old and I was a mere nine years old.

At first it was just gentle touches; he rubbed his large hands up and down my arms and gently massaged my shoulders. Then he would ask me if it felt good, and if I liked it and if I liked him and I always agreed. I thought I was a super star! I had this 20-something-year-old guy taking an interest in me and giving me attention. Who wouldn't like that?! With so many brothers and sisters, attention was often hard to come by. Over time, the gentle touches turned into taking my clothes off and his clothes off and making me touch him. I remember not understanding or knowing anything about what he was asking me to do, but I just did it. The touches evolved. He would make me suck on his penis as he pushed my head up and down until it would choke me. Then he would play with me, and stick his big fingers up inside me and ask me if that felt good. I would always say yes even when it hurt so badly that tears ran down my face. I always put on a brave face and shut off my feelings, emotions and conscience. He would kiss me and tell me he couldn't believe what a great kisser I was for being so young; I was all of nine years old.

He was always telling me what a great time we were having and I was scared to disagree and so it went. He told me that I could not tell anybody, that this was our secret and that he really liked me but nobody could find out about our special time. I always felt yucky and gross after those encounters and about the whole situation. I felt guilt for enjoying the attention and shame because I knew what he was doing to me was wrong and it hurt!

As the abuse continued, I began to feel dirty and I began to loathe his attention. I would hide, but he would look for me and tell my siblings to come find me because I was supposed to be cleaning the shop or something. The abuse continued off and on for about two years, maybe more. It usually took place at his parents' farm, in the corn fields behind my dad's shop, or in my dad's shop when nobody else was around. It was such a traumatic time for me that I cannot be exactly sure when or why it stopped and I never told anybody, so I really have no timetable for these events because everything from that time period of my life just runs together. All I know for certain is that this is when my world flipped upside down and my innocence was ripped away from me. The once fun, energetic, creative, imaginative little girl turned into a scared, secret holding child that felt alone, ashamed and always in fear. Later I would find out that this same man molested both my older sister and younger sister during the same time period. None of us talked to each other until we were adults about that abuse. There was so much fear and shame, we felt like we deserved it in some sick icky way. It is at this age that I became a master liar. I lied about my identity, I lied about my abuse, I lied to stay out of trouble, I lied because it was easier than risking telling the truth.

I wish this molestation/sexual abuse experience was an isolated one, but it would become just the first of many within the group and outside. I became a pro at painting on a smile and covering the shame, pain, fear and disgust with being loud, obnoxious and outrageous, an Oscar worthy overcompensation. Looking back, I realize those were coping mechanisms and cries for help, but no one saw that. Instead, they just saw a loud, energetic, disruptive, bad kid.

I was fondled and touched inappropriately by a boy within the cult over a summer when I was about eleven. I was summoned by Cultman on this particular summer to stay at the compound during summer break from school away from my family. This was not unusual; I had spent summers there before. During the week, Cultman would travel to see his children who were away at college on the east coast. I was left in the capable hands of his then caretaker, Dawn. My days were filled with weeding gardens, watering trees, clipping grass yards with scissors, cleaning the compound and any other menial tasks Cultman wanted done and that he had instructed Dawn to oversee. I also worshiped, prayed and studied each day in between work.

Lee was a teenage boy a few years older than me that was also spending the summer at the compound. Boys and girls were not allowed to talk or associate with one another, but we did work on projects or tasks together. Lee started whispering to me behind Dawn's back and we would sneak out and talk to one another at night or when we were walking to go to the bathroom or shower. Pretty soon Lee started telling me that he liked me. Then one day he pulled me into a back room at the house where we showered and he began kissing me and putting my hand down his pants as he rubbed my breasts. I kept saying "no" and tried to pull away, but he thought it was a game and told me to "shhhhhhh, someone might hear us."

In retrospect, I did like him, so I guess I figured that this is what people that liked each other did. I also realize now that because of the things I had already experienced with Danny, I romanticized this and made myself believe that it was okay even though I didn't feel comfortable or like it. And so the cat and mouse game began. Many times when he would try to touch me I just let him, because if I didn't fight or pull away it was over more quickly. But sometimes, I just wanted him to leave me alone, so I would fight and tell him no but to no avail. I did like the attention he gave me, but it came at a cost and the abuse was the cost.

That summer fling of torment came to an abrupt end because someone spotted us and reported us to Cultman. We did not know that we had been caught until Cultman came back that weekend and told me and Lee to meet him in the red carpet room. The scene that unfolded will forever be etched into my memory. Cultman was sitting Indian style, and I was sitting on my knees to his left and Lee on his knees to his right. He began asking Lee if he liked me and if he had done sexual things with me. I sat there staring at the floor and listened to Lee deny and lie over and over to Cultman. Cultman continued to question him, and he continued to deny everything. I was so scared about what was going to happen to Lee because that was one thing you never did, you did not lie to Cultman! The punishment was too great to even consider; in addition, lying to Cultman was sinning against God!

I began to cry, and then blurted out "Lee, just tell the truth!" Immediately Cultman's attention shifted towards me. "Marthee," (that's what Cultman called me), "tell Cultman what this bad boy did to you." He said it in an almost loving but a somewhat mocking tone. I began to give an overview of how Lee had told me he liked me and how he had touched me. Cultman began demanding details about where he touched me and how it felt. He wanted specifics and pressed on. "Did he go inside you? Did it hurt a little or did it just feel good?" I remember being absolutely mortified! I had never heard Cultman talk like this. It was gross and disgusting!

At the moment, I thought maybe Cultman was belittling and trying to humiliate Lee because he had lied, but with each question I became increasingly embarrassed and ashamed. I now realize that it was Cultman's own sick perversion, why else would you demand such details! And because I feared Cultman so much, I had no choice but to answer all questions and answer honestly. At the end of the tyranny of questions, Cultman told me I had done good to tell the truth and Lee was in big trouble for lying. I cannot be sure as I clearly have blocked that memory, but I am pretty sure that we both got severe whippings or some kind of physical discipline, which was common.

A lot of my physical abuse at the hands of Cultman runs together. I do remember that Lee was made to stick his nose to a pole in the basement of the compound for many, many weeks as part of his punishment. He was not allowed to go to the bathroom or eat without Cultman's permission. We were both publicly humiliated in front of all the Brethren during several meetings regarding this event. Cultman had a way of saying things that just made you cringe and want to hide under a rock. He would say things like, "Marthee is so dirty that only dirty filthy niggers want to be with her. And Marthee was begging for Lee boy to lie down with her. She just wants to make babies, and lay with every boy that will have her. Go Marthee, go open your legs, Lee wants some more!" And that is just the PG version of the things he would say. All of this absurdity and filth and I am all of 11 years old!

This type of humiliation caused such emotional torment and made me hate myself and feel so ugly, filthy, ashamed and useless at such a young age. It was some time before I was back in Cultman's good graces. Luckily at the end of the summer I went back home with my parents and siblings and was spared being subjected to this humiliation and judgment as consistently. That was the last summer that I spent at the compound until I permanently moved in when I was 18.

At around age eight, Cultman took a special interest in me. This was a great place to be, but a very dangerous place to be as well. I was physically disciplined much more than others but I was also given preferential treatment when it suited Cultman. When I speak of preferential treatment, I mean that Cultman would accept my paper towel rather than ones from others when he was cooking or if he touched something dirty.

Cultman was a very peculiar man and he was OCD about cleanliness. Growing up, the teenage girls in the group would follow him around holding a paper towel roll and just hoping that he would take their paper towel to wipe his brow, face or hands. It was looked at as such an honor for him to use something of ours and if he accidently touched us while he was grabbing for our paper towel that just made our day and made the other girls jealous. Preferential treatment also meant that I was sometimes served first to eat, or was allowed to go to the bathroom more frequently or allowed to clean Cultman's boots.

You see, members of the group were not free to touch Cultman because he was "holy," and if he was touched by a mere member he could be tainted or corrupted and no one would risk that! So the next best thing to touching him was to be able to touch something of his. So cleaning his boots was a huge honor and only a very select few were allowed to do it, and you had to be chosen. The preferential treatment did not last; it came and went as I got older and things within my life and the group changed.

Many times I wished that I could just be unnoticed by Cultman and fade into the background. The stigma of being Cultman's favorite saddled me and caused tension between me and my parents and siblings. The expectation of such a position was frankly to be Cultman's spy against my parents, siblings, fellow Brethren and their children. But the ramifications of such acts for those I reported on were public humiliation, verbal abuse, and/or physical abuse. But it seemed the more I was reporting on someone else, the safer I was and the more forgiving Cultman was to me when I misbehaved or sinned. This expectation was cyclical. I was threatened and forced to implicate my parents, siblings and others or else I would lose my privileged status with Cultman. He had cunning ways of asking questions and getting you to tell on yourself and or others for their shortcomings or if they fell out of line with Cultman's expectations and teachings. Cultman used isolation, manipulation, brainwashing, verbal, spiritual, sexual, physical and emotional abuse all as tactics to control us and to keep us in fear and under his reign.

To the best of my recollection, physical abuse at the hands of "Cultman" began around age seven and was ongoing. This was another way he controlled us. The smallest infraction would lead to torture or beatings with 2x4s, metal switches, extension cords, 3-foot wooden ladles, cattle prods, storage barrels, basically anything he could get his hands on when it was time for repercussions of the infraction.

Interesting fact, he never abused me in front of my family. I was generally taken into the kitchen, the red carpet room, and another back room or he waited until there were less witnesses. There were definitely Brethren's kids that witnessed my abuse and I witnessed theirs, but we never spoke to our parents or other adults about it.

CHAPTER 3

Moving Away

My dad's manufacturing business was bought out by a large corporation in North Carolina. My parents' sought counsel with Cultman, and for whatever reason my family was given permission to move. I am certain Cultman saw money signs around my dad so he let us go. In July of 1990 (when I was 12 years old), our family packed up my dad's business and our small farm house, loaded up one U-Haul and our 15-passenger van and moved to Chapel Hill, North Carolina. Moving was a big deal for my family. Families did not usually move that far away from the group where they would be unable to make the weekly trek to the compound. The move brought a considerable amount of freedom for my family that we had never experienced before, not to mention our new home was over three times as big as the small farm house that we left behind. In the farm house, my parents had a bedroom, the boys had a bedroom and the girls had a bedroom, adorned with bunk beds. I never remember feeling cramped; it was all we knew. The new house had five bedrooms and three bathrooms, talk about an upgrade! I distinctly remember the first week in our new home. My oldest sister was 19 and my youngest brother was 18 months. The new house was so spacious! For the first few days, many of my siblings and I all slept together in sleeping bags in one large room, because we didn't know how to be apart from one another or what to do with all this space! Slowly we all settled in and our new norm ensued.

We no longer went to the compound every weekend, and thus had time to do other things. Our whole lives really opened up. Cultman was concerned about us having too much freedom and instructed my family that we needed to listen to all the sermons on the speakerphone each Saturday and Sunday (oftentimes as many as six to eight hours). Cultman would have someone call us when he was ready to go to the meeting and then we would sit around the phone and listen to the entire meeting. At least when it was over we could go about our business. And if we had to go to the bathroom during the meeting time, we didn't have to ask for permission; instead, we just got up and went. We also didn't have to sit for endless hours on our knees, since Cultman couldn't see us. We sat however we wanted, but still on the floor, no couch or chair sitting as that would have been disrespectful. In retrospect, we had a semblance of normalcy once we moved to North Carolina. I say semblance with a little sarcasm because how normal could things really have been when we still dressed differently, ate differently, and spent our weekends huddled around the speakerphone listening to sermons for hours on end. My family still kept most of the rules of the group. We weren't allowed to have sleepovers, or go to the movies, or participate in school functions such as school dances, prom, etc. We weren't allowed to participate in school sports or any other extra-curricular activities because that was what people in the "world" did and we were taught we were different.

I felt different and was conscious of that feeling even more so once we moved to North Carolina. I felt like I lived and was stuck between two completely different worlds. I think it was because we did not have other families from the group around us anymore and because of our location we didn't visit the compound as often, so it was quite apparent that we were different. We seemed to not fit into the outside world, but we also didn't really fit in with the Brethren now because when we visited we were treated as that: visitors.

My family drove 19 hours one way to physically attend the weekend get-togethers at the compound four or five times a year. My parents were expected to drive straight through, no stops to rest. Only stops were made when we needed fuel. Refueling was our opportunity to use the restroom and stretch a little. Food was packed in the coolers in the van, and we all ate on the go. When we did visit Cultman and the Brethren, they treated us like outsiders, looking, pointing and picking on us, name calling. It was like my family took a hazing every time we visited. We had to be reinitiated back into the fold each time. Some of the Brethren's kids would flock to me and my brothers and sisters and ask questions. They were so curious about what it was like to be so far away and not come to the compound every weekend, and what was the world really like? Most of the families that were part of the group homeschooled their children so their kids were really cut off and isolated from society as a whole, and they were very naïve.

Outside of those infrequent trips to the compound, life was fairly normal (at least what I knew as normal). My brothers, sisters and I all went to public school. Going to public school was always a challenge. No one knew me really. Not even my closest friends had any clue who I was or what I was going through or why I did the things I did. Even though I was in public school, all aspects of my life and my family's existence were controlled and monitored by Cultman.

I was in the sixth grade and, as an extrovert, I did not have a hard time making friends. But for each friend I made it seemed there was always one that was picking on me or one of my siblings and I needed to protect them. Kids would ask us why we dressed the way we did, and why the girls' hair was so long, and what religion my family was, and why we had so many kids and on and on. Lying was easy for me, so I began fabricating and making up very creative stories to these types of unsolicited questions. When kids asked me what religion I was, I had various responses, one of them Hasidic Jews. I didn't even know what that meant, but I had heard about them one time and knew they dressed very modestly and had a very restricted diet so it just made sense. Plus, my family also didn't eat pork, pizza, pasta, candy, chocolate, peanut butter, shellfish and many other things, some of which I later found out that Jews do not partake in either. I knew that no one would say, "No you aren't" or question my answer so it was far easier for me to tell people that we were Jewish than tell them the truth (especially since I had no clue what my religion was or why we did the things we did). Frankly, the only thing I did know was that we did what we did because Cultman told us to. At a very early age, all of us kids were programmed that our group was a chosen people and we were meant to be different and we didn't want to fit in with the gentiles, plus no one on the outside would understand us so we didn't talk about it.

The isolation from the outside world was real. We weren't allowed relationships with our extended family because they weren't part of the group and they may try to brainwash us and turn us against Cultman and the group. It became easy to lie about my true identity, which was just one of the many secrets I hid.

From 13 to 18, my family said I was a problem child and a qualified rebellious teenager. I rebelled against my parents and the group rules. I began smoking, drinking, experimenting with drugs and having promiscuous sex. My parents would use Cultman as a crowbar to scare me straight when I was caught doing these things. Cultman was more than ever fibrously intertwined in our lives and still controlled my family even from 1100 miles away. When I was about 14 or 15, Cultman felt he was losing control of me so he demanded that I start calling him daily when I got home from school. There were no cell phones, and our home had three or four landline phones but all except one was in a public area. So each day, I would go into my parents' bedroom for privacy, kneel down on the floor in a praying position beside their bed, and call Cultman. Most conversations would go something like this.....

Me: This is Adam's sister Martha, may I speak to Cultman, please? (That is not what I called him at that time.)

Caretaker: Just one minute.

Cultman: Marthee?

Me: Yes, Cultman (in a scared half to death tone).

Cultman: Are you home from school now?

Me: Yes, Cultman.

Cultman: What are you going to be doing now?

I would then run down the list of what my afternoon looked like. Sometimes Cultman would ask if my parents were there, and what they were doing. It seemed like he asked that in hopes of catching them doing something that they weren't supposed to be doing. One time Cultman was not available until the evening and I had been calling for hours before I finally got a hold of him. I was not allowed to just call once. I had to keep calling until I reached Cultman. On this particular night, Cultman asked me what my parents were doing. I told him that they were in the bathroom together.

That weekend over the speaker phone during the meeting Cultman over and over belittled my parents saying that I had told him that they were taking showers together when none of us children had eaten, and basically the children were being neglected while my parents were in the shower playing teenager games. He said, "Aren't you two too old to be playing with one another, having sex and don't you have enough children?" His verbal venomous rant went on and on, belittling my parents and making everyone hearing the rant feel dirty and gross. I was mortified, and so were my parents, of course.

I knew what I had told Cultman and it was not what he was saying in the meeting, but I just assumed that it must be true about them in their spirit and that is what Cultman was honing in on. This incident was brought up numerous times over the next several years, and always nasty things were said about my parents regarding it. These afternoon nonsensical phone calls continued all through high school. The more rebellious I became, it was like Cultman bought into it. Cultman began pitting me against my parents. He would tell me that my parents didn't like me because I was Cultman's favorite. He would massage my ego and ask for dirt on my parents and siblings. If I did something wrong and my parents caught me, my dad would chase me around threatening to "take my head off" and then he would call and tell Cultman. I didn't like my dad's threats and occasional "belt lickings," but I was not scared of my parents. I was very scared of Cultman! Disappointing Cultman was far worse than getting a whooping with a belt or stick by my dad on the few occasions that it happened.

My rebelliousness and wrongdoings usually got turned around on my parents, and they would get rebuked for not being better parents. This in retrospect was completely unfair. My parents didn't feel like they had the power to be parents; they trusted Cultman to be in that role. This was how Cultman controlled everyone. Fear and making you feel that you were nothing without him. When my parents tried to parent, they were overridden by Cultman, and when they sought counsel from Cultman, they were shamed for being useless parents. It was a no-win situation!

From 14 to 16, I was repeatedly sexually abused by another member of the cult. His name was Aiden and he was about eight years older than me. He had taken a job in South Carolina and Cultman told him to come to our house in North Carolina on the weekends so that he could listen to sermons. It began like a boy crush. He would pay me attention and bring me candy or cigarettes, which of course we weren't allowed. Then slowly he got comfortable and started touching me. He would tell me that I couldn't tell anyone. He even gave me money sometimes to give him a blow job or to let him fondle my breasts or finger me. He was around a lot, and was always making a point to get me alone. It got to the point that I would lock my bedroom door to keep him from coming to get me during the night. If I forgot to lock it, he would sneak into the room that I shared with my younger sister and pick me up out of my bed and take me to the living room where he slept. He knew I wouldn't make noise because my parents' bedroom was right next door and they would wake up. So I would go along with whatever sexual thing he asked me to do so I could go back to bed. I began to hate his attention, and got scared and annoyed every time I knew he was coming because I knew what his visit would mean. This sexual torment only stopped when my sister woke up and witnessed Aiden breaking into our bedroom with a butter knife and picking my sleeping body out of my bed and carrying me out of the bedroom. I later found out that she followed us to the living room and witnessed the abuse. She asked me about it the next morning and I begged her not to tell anyone. I then told Aiden what my sister had seen and the abuse stopped. Because of the fear of being verbally humiliated and physically disciplined, neither I nor my sister ever spoke of this or the other horrific acts until late into my 20s after I escaped.

I knew at a very young age that I couldn't seek refuge in my parents or confide in them because they weren't allowed to be parents; they were in fact completely unaware of what was really going on. Cultman was intertwined in all parts of our existence! The way I dealt with these events was to become even more extroverted; I went out of my way to be louder and more absurd and I did anything to get attention. That was my protection mechanism. That was the way I hid my fear, hurt and shame. I didn't like anything about myself. I avoided the mirror because I felt fat, disgusting, ugly, and unclean, but no one would know it because I built walls of protection masked with fake positivity and endless energy early on that not even dynamite could break through.

During my teen years, I created many alternate egos and lived several different lives. I was constantly weaving my way in and out of things with one lie or another. Although I lived under my parents' roof, they truly had no clue what I was ever doing. I got my driver's license at age 16 and began to work as a waitress at a retirement community after school. For a least two or three years prior, I had been working at my dad's shop after school building furniture with my dad and siblings. All of us kids had a great role model in our dad when it came to work ethic, and the manual labor that most of us experienced at the cult compound reinforced such work ethic. We worked so we could give Cultman our tithe, but for me I worked so I could afford to do the things I wanted to do.

As soon as I got my license, I started sneaking out of the house regularly to meet up with friends, smoke pot, drink and have sex. I remember so many times that I would put my gray S10 pick up truck in neutral and roll it down our driveway until I was far enough away from the house that my parents would not hear it when I started it up, then I would jump in the truck and off I would go. When I returned, I pushed the truck back up the drive and snuck back into the house. During this stage, my parents loosened up with some of the cult rules and allowed us to have friends come over to our house, but never allowed them to spend the night. Numerous times, I hid my friends in my closet or under the bed in order for them to spend the night. Looking back I wonder what the hell they thought? I am certain I told them some kind of convincing lie in order to normalize the situation or made my parents out to be crazy, over-protective naysayers. My friends didn't know about my life at home (except what they were privy to observe), and my family didn't know about my life with my friends. I did a pretty good job of keeping those worlds separate. The only time that one or the other would get a small glimpse is when I would get caught in a lie. But even then, I was very convincing and I would tell another lie and usually get out of it.

Smyrna, my sister 17 months younger than me, was unfortunately dragged into a lot of my shenanigans. We always shared a bedroom. She was introverted, studious, and was easy to manipulate. I was loud, inconsiderate, didn't care about school and was labeled a troublemaker. For Smyrna, school came pretty easy, whereas, learning in general came very difficult for me, and frankly I was uninterested. Smyrna had pity on me and helped me with my homework and read out loud to me well into our teenage years. Essentially, she is the reason I have a high school diploma. I bullied Smyrna into doing things, and often used her as a scapegoat. In essence, I controlled her. I made her lie for me and cover for me, and all the while she looked up to me. We had a love-hate relationship. We joke that I loved Smyrna and she hated me.

It was a strange dichotomy because she saw me as the popular, cool older sister that was quite a rebel, but she was also annoyed with having to be the caretaker in our relationship. I was extremely needy and she was always having to pick up the pieces when shit hit the fan. In high school, teachers would call her out of class when I would have an allergic reaction, asthma attack, hyperventilate, or have a panic attack. Unfortunately, these things were common occurrences. I have many regrets about how I treated her in those years, but looking back I see clearly how it happened. I felt so out of control in my own life, and felt that my every move was controlled and scrutinized by the cult that I needed control over something, and that for me was Smyrna.

By my teenage years, I was already hiding so much trauma, pain, secrets and lies that honestly I don't know how I maintained sanity. God was definitely always looking out for me, but Smyrna was my in-the-flesh rock and whipping post. Our relationship had its ebbs and flows. Smyrna slowly let my outward corruption seep into her consciousness and eventually she loosened up and took on some of my rebel tendencies. For example, I would take scissors and cut my own hair, or give myself bangs. Or I would let a friend cut my hair; I knew I would get in trouble with my parents, but I didn't care. I knew they couldn't glue my hair back on, so in the end I would get what I wanted. I was tired of long hair, I always kept it just long enough that I would be able to put it in a bun when we took trips to the compound. Soon enough, Smyrna followed suit and began cutting her hair. Then in ninth or tenth grade I decided I was not going to wear skirts and blouses anymore to school. I had a job and was making money, so I started buying a new wardrobe. I would leave the house in the morning with a normal cult approved skirt and shirt, and then I would get in my truck and on the way to school I would change into shorts, jeans or whatever. I would stuff my skirt behind my truck seat and then on the way home I would pull it back out and put it back on before getting home. It wasn't long before I corrupted Smyrna into doing this as well. I remember one time that this type of sneakiness almost blew up in our face.

I had a bad asthma attack at school and per protocol the nurse called my sister. She was one grade behind me, and whenever I got sick or had an attack they always called her. On this particular day, the nurse wanted me to go to the hospital because I was not getting better after a regular albuterol nebulizer treatment. They wanted to call an ambulance. I asked them not to call the ambulance because my sister could just take me. Our mom worked at the hospital and I told the nurse that she would meet us there. See, that was the problem, our mom did work at the hospital and my sister and I were both wearing inappropriate clothing and if I was taken to the hospital in the ambulance my mom would catch me. So I volunteered my sister to take me so we could put our skirts on before getting to the hospital. For some reason, the nurse agreed to let us leave school and for my sister to take me to the hospital.

The only problem with this equation was my sister didn't have a license and had never driven a stick shift. In my ailing state and in between puffing on my inhaler, I gave Smyrna instructions on how to drive a stick shift. I instructed when to push the clutch and when to shift, etc. She actually did a fantastic job driving, until we came around the bend on a country road and saw a police roadblock set up in front of us on both sides. Oh SHIT! We were both so scared! She didn't have a license and I was sick! It was too late to change drivers or turn around because the cops would see us. By the grace of God, the roadblock was finished just a couple of cars ahead of us, and the cops waved us through.

Another time, Smyrna and I told our parents we were going to babysit, and I took Smyrna over to see her boyfriend because she couldn't yet drive legally. She did have her permit now, though. As she visited with her boyfriend, I sat on the porch and proceeded to get drunk. At some point I began to throw up and I proceeded to take my clothes off. She found me sometime later sitting on the steps of the porch in nothing but my shorts, leaned up against the railing moaning in a drunken stupor. She had to dress me, load me in the truck and then proceeded to drive us home.

There were many of these types of situations that I put Smyrna through that most of the time worked out for us. I definitely had a case of dumb luck. Then there were times that it just blew up in my face and Smyrna would have to let me take the fall.

One night I snuck out of the house and walked to the end of our road and my best friend Shanna picked me up and we headed to Burlington to meet up with some other friends. Cell phones were a very new thing and my parents bought me one to use only in case of an emergency. It looked like a brick with an antenna. I was out gallivanting with my friends when my cell phone rang. It was Smyrna. She whispered, "You better get your butt home. You are in huge trouble! They know you are gone!" I didn't have time to get the details from her. I just knew something had gone down and I needed to get home. With that phone call, our partying came to an abrupt halt and we started heading home. My sister called again to warn me that our dad had left in his car and was out looking for me. I knew I was in for it! I had Shanna drop me off at the very top of our road which is a good half mile from our house. I didn't want to risk Shanna running into my dad. Plus I had to get my skirt out of the mailbox and I didn't want my friends to see me do that. I put on my skirt and started running towards home. I saw headlights coming up behind me and I jumped into the woods to hide. As the car passed, I realized it was my dad. My heart was pounding and I had pretty much accepted my doom when my cell phone rang again. It was Smyrna again. She said that dad was back home and that he had just tried to call Cultman. My heart sank! I kept running towards the house and when the house came into view, every light was on and I could see lots of heads. It was about 2:00 in the morning and my actions had awoken the entire house. I snuck in the side door and ran into one of my brothers. He whispered, "You are in so much trouble!" Then I saw my mom. She just gave me a very angry look and said, "Martha, where have you been? Your father has been all over looking for you, and now he is on the phone with Cultman!" I knew all I could do was wait.

Soon enough, Dad got off the phone and came to the living room and saw me. He started screaming and yelling, and I took off running outside! This made him even madder! I can't remember which one of us got tired first and gave up, but eventually I accepted my beating, and then was told I needed to go call Cultman. I was so scared to call

Cultman especially when I knew I had done something really bad. I hated to get rebuked or disappoint Cultman. I can still remember that phone call like it was yesterday. Cultman got on the phone and said, "Marthee, where have you been?" I told him the truth that I had snuck out of the house and gone to Burlington to hang out with my friends. He asked if I had a boyfriend there. I said, "No." He asked what else we were doing and I told him just hanging out, listening to music, and smoking cigarettes. I began to cry and I expected to get verbally reprimanded! But instead, Cultman said, "Marthee, I know you don't like your parents but you can't do things like this. I was so worried! Cultman doesn't want anything bad to happen to you. Marthee, just don't do it again, ok?" I said, "Yes, Cultman," in between tears.

Cultman continued, "Now go to bed and forget this ever happened. If your parents ask, just tell them you have already talked to Cultman about it and you don't need to talk to them any further about it." And that's what I did. I came out of the room from talking to Cultman and walked straight into my room totally disregarding my parents that had been patiently waiting for me. I smirked climbing into bed. I won again!

I think back on incidents like this and wonder how my parents survived not being allowed to parent. I know now that this was Cultman's tactic of keeping us all in his control. By keeping himself firmly inserted in all of our business and lives, he stayed in control. My parents most likely thought that I had gotten in so much trouble from Cultman that they didn't need to punish me any further. He constantly played the kids against the parents and the parents against the kids. This was just another one of his mind control tactics.

My shenanigans and carefree life and doing whatever I wanted came to an abrupt halt seven days after I graduated high school. My parents were ordered by Cultman to bring me up to the compound. The way he sold it to my parents was that I was an out-of-control teen, defiled, and a disgrace to my family. My parents were told that I wasn't going to amount to anything in my life if I didn't get away from my friends and all the bad influences and get straightened out. The way he sold it to me was that I needed to get away from my parents because they didn't like me or understand me and I needed to come stay with him and get away from them. Little did I know that this would be the beginning of the next eight years of terror.

CHAPTER 4

Time to Cleanse

On Friday, June 20, 1997, we packed up the family and most of my cult approved belongings and drove from North Carolina to Wisconsin. This trip was different and the whole family knew it and felt it. Two siblings that were older than me had moved back up to Minnesota to go to college, but neither had been summoned by Cultman to come live in the compound. By the time of my move, both of my older siblings had moved away and no longer attended meetings although their allegiances were still to Cultman. We arrived at the compound and the weekend was just like any normal weekend that my parents and I had come to visit. All of this changed and my life became a living hell the minute my family packed up and drove away from the compound to return to North Carolina. The taillights of my family's van were still visible on the driveway leading away from the compound when Cultman pulled me aside and said in a belittling and disgusted tone, "Marthee, you are fat and ugly and the things you have done with boys and your body are disgusting, vile and you should be ashamed of yourself! You must repent. God doesn't like you and neither does Cultman! Marthee, don't you want to be cleansed, and forgiven?," he asked in a somewhat kind tone. Of course I said, "YES!"

I was almost in a weird way excited for this opportunity. I knew the things I had done, and I did feel dirty, ugly, ashamed and defiled. Cultman explained that I needed to detox my physical body. I was all for a detox, but I had absolutely no idea what was in store for me. I remember thinking how lucky I was to have Cultman care so much about me that he would want to find a way to cleanse me! After being told of my impending cleanse, Cultman proceeded to take me to my assigned living area. It was segregated from everyone else that lived in the compound. At any given time there were a handful of kids and young adults living at the compound. My designated spot in those early days was the prestigious real estate on the left-hand side of the stairs that lead up to Cultman's part of the compound.

Let me further describe my living quarters. No electricity, furniture, carpet, cabinets, or storage, just a cold 4x6 space that was plywood covered. There was zero privacy, as it was open to the main cooking kitchen. I plopped my things down and lined them up neatly against the side of the stairs. My belongings were minimal. A sleeping bag, an accordion, a small Rubbermaid box of toiletries, and a larger Rubbermaid box of "cult approved" clothes for all seasons. I had a duffle bag with my shower towels and a few other necessities, and that was it.

The following morning I was introduced to the rules of my cleanse. My first gallon of tang arrived and I was told by Neema, one of Cultman's caretakers, that she would be weighing me each morning. Each morning like clockwork my gallon of tang arrived and I was asked to step on the scale. Now, I didn't know much about a cleanse or fasting detox, but I thought three or four days, yeah I got this. But days dragged into weeks, and weeks into months. Each day, Neema would make me a gallon of Tang and that was all I was allowed to eat or drink. On three or four different occasions during this period I was given a few leaves off of a head of iceberg lettuce. That was a true treat! Cultman traveled away from the compound during the week so when he returned on Friday I was always nervous. He would look at my weight loss recordings and if I didn't lose as much weight as he thought I should, he would get very angry and accusatory and demand to know whose food I was stealing and where I was sneaking food from! On many occasions he would try to beat a different answer out of me. I was beaten with electrical cords, two by fours, wooden spools, or whatever he could get his hands on. The truth was I wasn't getting food from anywhere else! I was slowly being starved to death.

There were a few other children living in the compound at the same time that I was, but they would have been scared to death to sneak me food for fear of repercussions from Cultman. I remember in one particular meeting he was talking about how I wasn't losing enough weight and told me to get up during that meeting and run up and down a flight of stairs until he said stop. There were 25 to 30 stairs and it was a steep incline. I ran up and down those stairs for what seemed like forever. I am certain that it was until he felt like he had broken me. If I slowed down, he would make fun of me and tell me to start running.

As the months passed, I became more and more weak. I remember when Cultman was present I would try to stand up straighter and look okay, but it became more and more challenging. During the week when Cultman was not around, the children around me were always checking on me, and I remember a few times they went and got Neema because I didn't look good. Neema would tell Cultman I wasn't feeling well and Cultman would say I was faking it.

My nearly five-month starvation finally came to an end when my organs shut down and I blacked out. For a couple of days prior to my black out, I remember I had no energy and could not urinate which was good because I was not able to make the long walk to the neighbors' house. I have no recollection for how long I was blacked out. I was not taken to get medical attention as this would have drawn negative attention to the cult. Rather, Cultman summoned a doctor within the cult to nurse me back to life. I can't remember much about that time other than I was given baby food, Geritol vitamins, and some other medicine and still I felt sick all the time and for a long time. Eating and drinking were not enjoyable; it was more like a chore, and it was often painful. It was like my body just had forgotten how to digest anything. My stomach cramped and my head hurt and it took a long time before my bowels began working properly again. In total, I lost about 80 pounds and was down to 101 pounds at a mere 5 feet 4 inches tall. I was skin and bones.

My parents came to visit for Thanksgiving break that year. I still was not eating properly but I knew I had to act normal in front of my family. I remember the look on my mom's and my sister's face the first time they saw me during that visit. It was a look of sheer horror! I am sure they were thinking what in the world has happened to Martha? I looked emaciated, and sickly. My parents would not dare question what had happened to their daughter because I was under the careful eye of Cultman, what could possibly go wrong. Just as all the educated fellow Brethren that came each weekend and saw me getting skinnier and sicklier and never asked questions or said a word, rather they just watched it happen. And when Cultman would say in the meeting, "Look how fat and ugly Marthee is. She is stealing food from somewhere. She must be!" They all agreed. When it was all over, no one was told that I passed out or nearly died. It was just life as usual. The doctor I am sure never told anyone that she was in the back taking care of me and how close to death I was when she was summoned.

But with all that being said, ironically, I was never angry about this cleanse. I thought God was angry with me and I knew I had sinned and

I fully understood this was my penance. I even thought that God had allowed me to come face to face with death to show me how bad I had really been and how unworthy I was to live and have Cultman looking out for me and my life.

That year for Thanksgiving, Cultman made a ton of baked turkeys, mashed potatoes, sweet potatoes, etc. When it was time to eat, each family spread out a black garbage bag on the floor and Cultman would come around and hand out food on top of the garbage bag. I was so excited because I was sitting with my family but also because I had not gotten to eat food like this for so long and the smell was just about unbearable. I just wanted to eat! Cultman first handed out the turkeys, then the fixings. This was a very long process and no one dared to eat until everyone was served and Cultman had prayed over the food. I am pretty sure I was drooling as the feast was placed in front of my family! Cultman saw this, and suddenly told me to get up and go back to my spot, that I was not going to be eating with my family. He proceeded to demoralize me and tell everyone I was gluttonous and didn't deserve to eat with my family.

I was absolutely devastated as I hurried back to my spot. I sat on my sleeping bag and just began to cry, blaming myself for having a bad spirit of gluttony. I couldn't believe I had gotten so close to some real food and then had it snatched away from me. As I look back on the incident, I realize that the reason that Cultman did this was not because I was gluttonous but because Cultman realized that my body was not ready to digest this type of food and it would have made me very sick in front of my family so he needed to remove me before this happened.

Cultman could do no wrong in my eyes and in the eyes of the Brethren. We propped him up, honored, respected and revered him, and never questioned him in any way, shape or form. What he said went, no matter how ludicrous and ridiculous it sounded or appeared.

This was the beginning of the next eight years of my life. So much of what occurred is somewhat of a blur and I have still blocked out some of the details, but by and large it was the most difficult, scary, painful and humiliating time of my life.

In the spring of 1998, Cultman allowed me to enroll at the University of Wisconsin at Green Bay. Although I never liked or did well in school up to that point, and I had barely graduated high school, I was very excited about attending college. Mostly because it would get me out of the compound. Initially, I was denied. I appealed my denial and explained my learning disabilities and my desire for higher education and I was miraculously admitted on probationary status. Which basically means, they really shouldn't have admitted me but someone was feeling generous and was willing to give me a shot, since I had gone through all the trouble of appealing the denial. Probationary status meant that I had to maintain a 2.5 grade point average or higher for my freshman year or I would be kicked out. Because of my diagnosed learning disabilities, I was granted tutoring, extra time for exams and other helpful accommodations at no extra charge.

It turned out that I really enjoyed college and actually did very well. School work was an escape for me, and it kept my mind occupied. When I would get back to the compound in the evenings, I would huddle up under the nightlight and study. The night light was essential since we were not allowed to use the overhead lights when Cultman was not there. I have so many memories under that night light studying, drawing, writing, coloring, crying and praying. It wasn't an option to not do well in college. Cultman demanded to see my report cards as soon as I got them. If my grades weren't up to his standards, there were repercussions. Luckily, I never had to find out what the repercussions would be for this particular short-fall because I maintained mostly A's with an occasional B all through college.

Repercussions/beatings/parking/sticking nose to a pole/public humiliation were a regular part of life during my first few years living in the compound. There was a punishment for just about anything you could imagine. If I got caught talking to someone I wasn't supposed to, or if I was seen talking to a boy at school, or if I overslept, or if I fell asleep during a meeting, or if I took too long in the bathroom or shower, or if my blouse was deemed too tight or short, and on and on, punishment ensued. I could handle most punishments except for the beatings and the public humiliation. I became immune to the others early on. It was the only way to survive.

The beatings, I would just take it and then break down afterwards, never in front of Cultman. I think this frustrated him, so he would continue to chase and beat me. As I think back, he was waiting and hoping I would submit, but that was never my personality. I remember my family came to visit one time and I was so excited because I missed them tremendously. Smyrna and I were showering together in the communal showers and she saw that I was bruised head to toe. She asked me, "What on earth could you have done to deserve that, Martha?" I replied, "I got caught talking to a boy at school." She was flabbergasted! Another time a fellow Brethren's daughter saw me in the shower area and noticed that I had unacceptable underwear on. During a Sunday morning meeting, she stood up and reported to Cultman about my underwear. Cultman asked me to bring all of my underwear to the meeting room to show him. Now remember, this is in front of probably over 200 people! How embarrassing! I was totally humiliated as I showed each pair of my underwear and he approved or disapproved all the while verbally belittling me and my family with insults such as, "Why would Marthee want such underwear, is she looking for someone to lay down with?," of course insinuating that the reason I had chosen to buy bikini cuts instead of full cuts was because I was hoping that would help me find someone to have sex with and no other reason! I think back on some of these occurrences and think how and why did I stay as long as I did?

CHAPTER 5

Runaway Girl

I tried running away with a boy in December of 1998, but that turned into another nightmare. The boy's name was Ebenezer, Eb for short. He had left the cult several years before, but his family was still an active part of the group. He came back to the group in the fall of 1998, but was pretty much a non-participating part of the group which means that he followed most of the rules but did not come to meetings or spend much time in the compound. His father and I spent a lot of time together because we were assigned to a lot of the same manual projects. He was a woodworker and that is how my father started out, so I think Cultman assumed that I had the talent as well.

During that fall, Eb's father kept telling me that Eb wanted to settle down and get married and that he was interested in me. This type of conversation was totally against the rules. The protocol for such an arrangement was if a young man was interested in a young woman, the young man would go to Cultman and ask for permission to marry the young lady, not to date or court, but to marry her. This was not a common occurrence, marriages usually happened when Cultman assigned two people to do so. When Eb's father told me of Eb's plan to ask Cultman to marry me, I was extremely nervous but excited. I saw it as an escape! Eb was going into some kind of military thing, I am not sure which branch or even that this was true, but he was going to be moving to Arizona. When I heard this, I saw him as my ticket out, even if I had to get married to do it! So Eb did ask Cultman, and Cultman told him it would never work out, and basically no. Cultman also told him what a bad, filthy girl I was and that he didn't really want me for a wife. But by this time, Eb started having feelings for me, and told his dad that he thought he was falling in love with me. I did not feel the same, but I led on as I did because I saw him as my ticket to freedom!

Since Cultman turned down Eb's proposal, he and I started hatching a plan to run away. Eb would come down and talk to me when his father and I were working together. I am pretty sure that Eb's father knew about our plans but he never ratted us out to Cultman. Eb's dad was one of my father's friends and both joined the cult around the same time and hence he had a soft spot in his heart for me and my wellbeing.

I think that Eb's dad really wanted to see me with his son because he and my dad had always had a mutual respect and friendship even though that was not allowed once they joined the group. They had also done a business venture together years before and although it didn't work out they always had a special place in their hearts for one another.

Sneaking around was kind of fun! I remember the first time Eb hugged and kissed me on the lips. This was forbidden on so many levels! On this particular night, we were down in the Annex spraying varnish on some cabinets and we snuck away while his dad was busy spraying the doors and that's when it happened. As we snuck behind some shelving units, he grabbed and pulled me close in a tight embrace, and then very abruptly planted a kiss on my lips and then smiled from ear to ear. I felt like a young teenager getting her first kiss rather than an almost 20-year-old that was just yearning for attention.

After that kiss, I did grow to really like Eb. I fantasized about life with him, and what that would be like in Arizona. When I would get scared or worried about the what if's, I always reminded myself that if we as a couple didn't work out that at least I would be out of the compound if our plan worked.

After a couple of weeks of planning, we decided that the night we would get me out of the compound would be Wednesday, December 23, 1998. There was a reason that we picked that particular day. Wednesday was a group prayer night. Cultman was gone to visit his family on the east coast and all the families that were local would come and gather at the compound on Wednesday evenings to sing and pray for a couple of hours. Everyone would be in the meeting room which would allow me to sneak my things out of the other side of the compound without anyone noticing. The appointed night came. Eb never came to meetings, so we only had to worry about one of us getting out of the compound without drawing any attention. I went to the meeting just like everyone else, but then after about an hour or so I got up and left like I was going to go to the bathroom or something. Remember, the bathroom is at least a quarter of a mile away, so it takes some time to get there and get back. Since Cultman was not there, we could go to the bathroom if we needed to. I had moved some of my things outside so I didn't have to make so many trips back and forth to the compound. I was nervous as I stepped outside, was someone watching me, was someone going to catch us? Was Eb going to be waiting for me where we had planned? I walked up to the road just as Eb pulled up to the gate at the entrance of the long road that runs beside the compound. I grabbed a load of my things and ran to his truck and threw them in the back. I ran back quickly for another load. After just a few minutes and a couple of trips, all of my things were loaded and I jumped into the cab of Eb's truck and we took off.

We sat in silence for what felt like forever. Finally when we got out of town, he pulled over to properly secure my things in the back of his truck. When he got back into the cab, he said in a low tone, "We did it. We are free." I smiled. It just seemed too good to be true. I remember asking, "Where are we going?" Although we had planned my escape, we had never really talked about what we would do once we had me out of the compound. He told me that there was someone that he wanted me to meet, and that since it was just a couple of days until Christmas we were going to go first to Slayton, Minnesota, to meet his grandfather, his dad's father.

We talked most of the rest of the way to his grandfather's house. We really just got to know each other. Even though we practically grew up together since both of our families were in the cult, we knew nothing about one another. Cultman kept it that way, especially if it was girls and boys. If you got caught even talking to a boy, there was guaranteed to be a grave punishment to follow.

After driving five or six hours, we arrived at his grandfather's. The house was dark and quiet, which was understandable because it was probably around 1am or so. We went in and went straight to bed. I remember we shared a twin bed in a bedroom on the second floor of his grandfather's creaky old farmhouse. Sometime during the night I heard voices and I froze. The first thought that went through my head is that they had found me. They, being Cultman's henchmen (Brethren's sons that are sent to bring people back when they run away or do something wrong). I lay there paralyzed, unable to move and barely breathing. Then suddenly the bedroom door opened and in the door I could see Eb's little brother, Abe. I began to shake Eb to wake him up. When he awoke, I pointed to the door, as if to say look who's here! Eb said, "Oh, you guys made it, where's dad?" I was shocked! His family was in on this? They knew we ran away together? The truth would unravel later. Eb told Abe to go to bed and that we would see them in the morning.

I didn't sleep much the rest of the night. I lay awake wondering who else knew where I was and how long it would be before the henchmen arrived to bring me back. I was scared to go back; I knew I would be severely punished. That night I promised myself no matter what I was not going back, I would run and run if I had to, but I was not going back.

The next morning Eb and I went downstairs to the smell of pancakes. We arrived in the kitchen and there sat his grandfather, father, sister and two brothers. We ate pancakes and sat with the family. I remember thinking, this is so crazy! Here I ran away, and now I am sitting here with Eb's family like it's just a regular Thursday! His dad told us that Cultman knew we were gone, but his dad had told Cultman that he knew nothing. I remember being shocked that his dad had lied to Cultman. You just didn't do that! He told us that we needed to get back on the road before Cultman called again because he would have to tell Cultman that we were at the grandfather's house since the children had seen us. Right after breakfast, we said goodbye to the family and went outside to get in the truck and hit the road.

His dad followed us outside. Eb came to the passenger side door like he was going to open the cab door for me, and knelt on one knee and pulled a ring out of his pocket and asked me to marry him. I said, "Yes," although I don't think I really even knew what I was agreeing to. I just wanted to hit the road before anyone could stop us. His dad watched the whole thing. I turned and saw him and he seemed so happy. He said, "Congratulations, I am happy for you two. Now get out of here!" I think his dad legitimately wanted his son and me to be happy and he knew we would not be happy within the group since Cultman said no to us being together.

We began driving again. I had a huge pit in my stomach; I couldn't help but think that this was not going to end well. My thoughts raced. I tried to override them but I kept imagining the worst but simultaneously hoping and praying for the best! We talked and he tried to calm my nerves by telling me all the things he had planned for our future. I went along with his plans and tried to act excited, but in my mind I knew I wasn't going to marry him and that once I could make some money I would leave him and start my own life.

We stopped driving that night, which was Christmas Eve somewhere in Nebraska. We got a hotel for the night and unpacked our things. I called Smyrna to let her know that I had run away and to see if she knew if people were looking for me yet. By this time, Smyrna was no longer in the group and had very little to do with my family because she had chosen a boyfriend over the group so she had practically been blacklisted. Because of this, I knew I could call her and she wouldn't rat me out. She was so happy to hear from me, but I could tell by her voice that she knew something. She said that Cultman had called her already and was looking for me, and asked her if I had contacted her yet. I could tell she was afraid for me.

That night was difficult for many reasons. Time seemed to stand still as my fear of getting caught and being brought back grew exponentially. To add to my fears, Eb forced himself on me. I think he saw me as his property because he had put a ring on my finger. The details of the actual incident escape me, but the memories I do have is that I felt dirty and angry that night and the next morning. Why did he have to do this? But one thing the incident did clarify for me was that I knew without a shadow of a doubt that we would not be together! Once I was safely away from the cult, I would then leave him as well. But I knew that I had to calculate my moves because I had no money, no vehicle, and had no clue where I was.

The next day neither of us spoke of the incident. We began driving again. It was Christmas Day and I remember there were not very many people on the road. The tension was very thick and our conversation was very light, which was much different from the two days before. We drove for several hours before stopping somewhere in Colorado for dinner and to get a hotel. We ate dinner at Shoney's and I remember thinking I just can't do this. I can't go through with this. I was angry at Eb and I was scared to death for my life. I was remembering all the stories of people that had run away and how their lives had been ruined, and they would come back to Cultman begging for forgiveness. I remember thinking Eb forcing himself on me was my punishment because I had run away from Cultman. I knew what I had to do.

When we got to the hotel room, I told Eb I was going to relax and asked him to unload the truck. As soon as he left, I fell to my knees, said a prayer and picked up the phone and called Cultman collect. One of his caretakers answered the phone and as soon as she heard it was me, she accepted the charges and said they would go get Cultman. Cultman came on the phone and I remember just crying and begging for his forgiveness for running away. At first Cultman was silent and just let me cry and beg. Then he became very kind, and started asking for details, where were we, had I eaten, what had we done, where we had stayed, and so many more. I began to pour out the details and then Eb started banging on the door for me to let him in. Cultman told me to ignore him. I told Cultman that Eb had asked me to marry him, and Cultman told me to take off the ring and spit on it and go to the hallway and throw it at him. I did this, and I saw Eb slide down the wall and start crying. I knew he had figured out what I had done.

I went back in the room and closed the door and went back to the phone. Cultman started telling me that he was going to buy me a train ticket or plane ticket and bring me back, since I had told him the truth and realized what I had done was wrong. After some time, he asked to speak to Eb. I went out in the hallway to get him. He was still sitting there crying hysterically. I told him in a very cold tone that Cultman wanted to speak to him. He looked so scared. He came to the room and got on his knees and picked up the phone.

I don't know what Cultman said to him. All I heard Eb say was, "I am so sorry. I am sorry, Cultman," over and over again. Then, "Yes, yes Cultman," and then he handed me the phone.

Cultman told me that I was to drive Eb's truck and bring myself back. I was not to let him drive because he would turn the other way and/or hurt me if I fell asleep. I was also instructed that I was not to stop for anything except for gas. And each time we stopped for gas, I was to find a payphone and call Cultman to give an update. Cultman also told me not to talk to Eb because he would try to change my mind.

We loaded the truck back up and I started driving. Eb sat beside me and cried and cried and cried. Then he would become angry because I wouldn't talk to him, and he would scream and yell and I just continued to drive. My head and heart were calloused and on auto pilot. I couldn't bear to allow myself to feel anything, or I would crumble. I hated hearing him cry, but I felt he had done it to himself. If he hadn't forced himself on me, we would still be heading to Arizona. During his fits of crying and anger, he did apologize and just said that he had let his lust get the best of him and he was so sorry. Unfortunately, it was too late. What was done was done, and now I was headed back to the compound.

I drove and drove, and each time I stopped to fill up, I called Cultman. The conversations were very quick and Cultman would urge me to get back on the road. After several of these stops, and 22 hours later, we pulled back into the compound driveway. I rang the doorbell to tell Cultman I was back. Reality hit when I rang the doorbell. My stomach was in knots, and although it was the middle of winter, I felt flushed and sick. I was so scared to see Cultman; I knew that although

Cultman had been kind on the phone there was going to be hell to pay for my wrongdoings.

Cultman came to the door and told me to go downstairs and told Eb to leave the property and never come back, and threatened that if he did come back that the cops would be called. After four days of running, I returned to my existence in the compound; a sleeping bag in the back corner of the room adjacent to the meeting room on the cold concrete with no lights and a terrible, dingy mildew smell. I no longer resided by the stairs as I had been demoted to the big public room for some infraction prior to my running away. One of the first repercussions from this incident was that I was banished from sitting in the meeting room with the other Brethren's daughters during meetings. I had to sit outside the meeting room with the mothers that were nursing or had children that were too young to sit still during the lengthy meetings. I was filthy and defiled and if I sat next to other girls my filthy spirit could jump on them. Or even worse, if I accidently touched them, they would become a whore like me! I wasn't worthy to sit in the same room with all the other Brethren.

Now as I look back, that room was filled with sinners, they just didn't get caught! Cultman also of course publicly embarrassed me week after week, and said how dirty and filthy I was and told everyone the things I had done when I ran away. The Brethren were instructed to treat me like I had a scarlet letter or as if I was tainted. And so they did. This made me feel dejected, miserable, and I felt so lonely, but I felt that I deserved it. Some of the kids would find turkey and duck poop and put it in my shoes. Others spit on me and called me names. All of this was terribly hurtful and damaging to my psyche, but I thought I had brought it on myself.

A couple of months after returning from my four-day excursion, Cultman made an announcement in a Sunday morning meeting. I remember all too clearly this particular Sunday. My family was visiting and that was the first time I had seen them since before I had attempted to run away. I was sitting on the outside of the meeting room as I had done since my return when Cultman brought the meeting to a halt and said that the Lord had made known that in order to be forgiven for running away and defiling myself that all of my possessions should be burnt with fire and my head would be shaved. My heart leaped for joy! I was so excited! Cultman said I would be forgiven; I didn't even really hear the rest of what he was saying nor did I care! I was happy to hear there was a way for me to be forgiven. The enormity of this announcement did not have time to settle in, rather my mind started going a million miles an hour. My head was going to be shaved! What would everyone at school think? I was already an outcast, now I would have to go to school with my head shaved! And what do you mean by all my possessions? Like everything? The answer to this came as he explained how this would all be done. All of my things would be taken to the burning brush pile, and he told my mom that she would take me to get all new essentials. And so it was. That was February 14, 1999.

I remember that day all too clearly. I watched all of my things being taken to the burn pile and then my mom and I went to Walmart and bought me new necessities, a sleeping bag, toothbrush, shampoo, underclothes, clothes, towels, etc. Upon my return, I was taken to the neighbor's house so that one of the Brethren could shave my head as he had been instructed by Cultman. I remember that when he finished shaving it, it was a very, very short buzz cut and he said to me, "We better show Cultman." We did and Cultman said, "No, no, no, it needs to be shaved completely like a woman shaves her legs."

Once my head was shaved to the Cultman approved standard, Cultman instructed me to go take a shower and anoint myself with olive oil and pray and ask for forgiveness. I did exactly as I was instructed.

I felt a sense of relief as I got out of the shower and dried off with a brand new towel and put on my new clothes. There were not many cult approved clothing options at Walmart, so we bought what we could. Cultman was not pleased, so he instructed one of the Brethren's wives to sew me new clothes. The following weekend I had three new sets of cult clothes.

Once my things were burned and my head was shaved, it seemed that the banishment was lifted. I was no longer treated as badly and Cultman actually started giving me preferential treatment again. Cultman continued to instruct my head to be shaved on a monthly basis for the next fifteen months. I remember once asking Cultman to please stop having my head shaved, and he told me that I was to have my head shaved until the Lord returned. Each time my head got shaved, I didn't fight it, but I began to feel a hatred growing inside of me.

People in school and at my work thought I was very sick and having chemo or something. I just let them think this because that was easier for them to believe than if I would tell them the truth. A few months later, I told Cultman that people at school and work were very worried about me because they thought I was sick, and could I please stop having my head shaved. Cultman told me to "Do whatever you want; you are going to hell anyway." And that's how the head shaving stopped.

CHAPTER 6

Fudge & My Guardian Angel

In May of 2000, during another Sunday morning meeting, Cultman proclaimed that once again the Lord had made something known to him regarding me. This time it was that I was to manage the first business that the group had purchased. The next day I quit my job and dropped my classes at the University and did as I was told. I went to run the cult's gift and fudge shop. The shop was located about two miles from the compound in a beautiful historic all brick one room schoolhouse. I was told that I was just needed for the summer to get the business up and running and I would be able to go back to school in the fall. Fall came and I asked to return to school. Cultman said the store needed me, and no one would know what to do, as I had been the only one working at the store since the beginning. So I was never allowed to go back to school.

I worked at the fudge house for the next four years. This entailed 12-20 hour work days, 365 days a year with not one cent of compensation. I never had a day off in the four years that I managed that business and I never received one single penny for all the hours I worked. No sick days, vacation days, health insurance, no compensation at all. The shop was never successful, mostly because the stigma of it having to do with the cult not many locals would dare shop there. The occasional sale came from a tourist or someone that happened to be passing by and took interest in the historic building turned fudge shop.

On a great day, we would have five to ten sales, and on a normal day there were less than five sales. You are probably wondering how the business stayed afloat with such minimal profits. The answer is, all labor was free, and the majority of the sales of fudge were purchased by the Brethren on the weekends. Which in itself is ironic and humorous because fudge was on the forbidden list until it wasn't. Cultman saw there was profit to be made at the expense of the Brethren, so he changed his own rules to suit the new situation. Also, most weekends from spring to fall were spent with groups of the Brethren's daughters going around Wisconsin and Minnesota to fairs and other organized events where they would peddle the fudge. These were the main ways that the fudge shop made profit.

On one of the first days the shop was open, an older local man and his family stopped by to check out the store and buy some fudge. The older man was so friendly and he and I chit chatted while his daughter and granddaughter shopped. He told me that he had just moved to the area to be closer to his family and that they were so excited to see that the shop had opened less than a mile from his daughter's house. I remember him telling me on that first day that he saw something special in me, and that I was like a beaming ray of sunshine! The compliment felt so good, but so awkward. I was not used to getting compliments and for no reason. From the first time we met, he really saw me…with his heart and immediately took a liking to me. I came to call this gentle soul Papa.

Papa was short, stocky and physically strong for his age. He had silver hair, glasses and an endearing smile. He was always dressed impeccably with slacks, dress shirt and a tie, bow tie or bolo tie. He frequented the fudge shop almost daily during my tenure. Papa and I became very close. He felt like family! He was very kind with a generous spirit, a great listener and he loved God!

His wife was in a local nursing home suffering from Alzheimer's dementia. He was a lonely old man and always told me that his daily visits to my store brought him joy. He would go to the nursing home each morning to eat breakfast with his wife and then go back again in the evening to eat dinner with her. In between those times, he would come visit me at the shop, sometimes staying for a couple of hours, sometimes staying for a few brief minutes. Papa was the closest thing that I ever had to a grandpa. He would tell you that he was instantly drawn to me and that he felt that we both filled a hole in each other's hearts.

In those four years, I learned so much about Papa and his family and in turn about myself. I trusted Papa, and shared truths about my life that no one else had ever been privy to. One of the most important things that Papa taught me about was Jesus. Papa was a good Christian man. He lived and breathed the Bible and God's word. He lived the commandments and shared the message of Jesus's love and mercy wherever he went.

I remember the first time that he started sharing with me about Jesus. Papa asked me, "Martha, do you know Jesus?" My response, "Of course I do." Papa said to me, "Do you believe Jesus loves you?" I remember thinking what kind of crazy question is this? How could Jesus possibly love this sinful, dirty, ugly person such as me? Papa could see the hesitation, and interrupted my self-loathing train of thought. "Well, Martha," he said, "Jesus does love you and wants to be your Lord and savior and his friend."

I was absolutely discombobulated! Why in the world did Jesus want to be my friend? All I had ever been taught was that the Lord was to be feared and revered. Growing up in the cult I had never been told about the love, grace or mercy of Jesus or of his desire for a friendship with me. I had only learned that I was never good enough and that God was never happy with me and that he was a jealous God visiting the iniquities of the fathers upon the children from generation to generation. Brimstone and fire was my ending because of my sins!

Papa began to witness to me and I began to question all of the things I had grown up with. Papa was so sincere and told me over and over, "Jesus loves you, Martha, and he has forgiven you so you need to forgive yourself." With all of that being said, I always considered myself a Believer. I feel like I had a connection with God at a very young age even if I didn't really understand what that meant. I prayed all of the time, and I sought comfort from the tragedies of my life in the only thing I knew: weeping and prayer. But the thought of Jesus being my friend was asinine. Papa patiently continued to teach and introduce me to new ways of thinking about God and my views slowly did begin to change. What if God didn't despise me? What if God loved me? What if he had forgiven my sins? Papa's sharing opened up so many questions, and I often pondered them wondering if God loving me was truly possible? Could God "love a wretch like me"?

Papa came to the shop one day after we had spent nearly a year getting to know each other and said, "Martha, I have a question. Now please don't feel like you have to tell me anything that you don't want to, but you know that you can trust me and anything that you tell me will not be repeated." I swallowed hard. I knew where this was going. I was sure that he had finally heard something in town about my ties with the group and he was here to ask me about it. My intuition was spot on. He began to ask whether the shop was owned by the cult or if it was indeed owned by a lawyer from Minnesota which was the cover story I was instructed by Cultman to say if anyone ever asked this question.

I decided to be honest or at least partially. This was a very hard thing to do when your whole life is spent telling one lie after another. I told him yes that the group owned it, and he began asking me a litany of questions about the group and about Cultman. He was so interested and non-judgmental.

Papa had indeed begun to hear the rumors in town that the business was part of the cult and his curiosity had gotten the best of him. He orchestrated his questions carefully prying for the inside scoop but when I began to resist he dropped it. I sugar-coated just about everything after being honest about the ownership of the shop. I sold the group in a very positive light, and told him how proud I was to be chosen to run the shop and how great Cultman was. Towards the end of that conversation, Papa asked me if there was any way for him to meet Cultman. I told him that Cultman was a very busy man and didn't take meetings very often, but I would ask. I did follow through and asked. To my amazement, Cultman agreed to meet Papa. The shop had been under surveillance and it had been brought to Cultman's attention that Papa was spending a lot of time at the shop with me. Cultman had asked me about it on numerous occasions and had indicated that as long as he was buying fudge he could come as often as he wanted.

Papa ended up meeting with Cultman on a couple of different occasions. Cultman said he found Papa to be an interesting man with a heart for the Lord. Papa said that he found Cultman to be a peculiar guy that he could not really put a finger on what he believed, but seemed very nice and genuine. From what Papa told me, they discussed religion, some politics and of course our fudge. It always really intrigued me that Cultman had agreed to meet up with Papa. Ordinarily Cultman did not take meetings with outsiders unless it was a lawyer, banker or business opportunity, rather he would send one of his representatives. Cultman never just met up with a "heathen" because they asked. I think it had something to do with making sure he knew who was spending so much time with me, but also Cultman knew that Papa was good publicity. Papa was a walking billboard for the fudge shop. He raved to anyone that would listen about our fudge and gifts.

Papa began to slowly and painfully peel away my layers of distrust. He saw me when I was happy and when I was sad. He comforted and prayed for me when all I wanted out of life was to get married and have a family and it wasn't happening for me. I was patiently waiting for Cultman to assign me a husband, but it never happened. I struggled with this for a long time. I didn't understand why Cultman wasn't allowing me to get married. The truth, at least in my head, was that I was defiled, and I had sinned against God, therefore unworthy of happiness. I shared these thoughts and emotions and many others with Papa. He would pray with me and remind me that everything was in the Lord's time and that I needed to be patient.

I found my sister Smyrna on the internet in August of 2004. I had not seen or spoken to her in over five years. I began secretly calling her. Making this kind of phone call was very tricky. All of the lines were connected to the compound, so at any time someone in the compound could pick up and hear my conversation which was done routinely. I figured out a line that was not able to be picked up from anyone in the compound and that was the line for the internet. All I had to do was unplug the internet and plug in a phone and I had a private line.

I called my sister many times before I actually reached her. Each time I would call her, my heart would beat wildly and I would pray that she would pick up. After several failed attempts, I finally left a message on her answering machine. All I said was, "Smyrna, if you are there, pick up." I would later find out that Smyrna played and replayed that message and couldn't believe it was me. She answered the next time I called.

We had many heated conversations where she told me that I was in a cult and why couldn't I see that! I became so torn. I missed her so much and by this time several of my brothers had also left the group and I just missed my family. This pushed me to confide in Papa the truth about even more of my past and present. That specific conversation is forever cemented into my memory. Papa and I sat on the indoor entrance steps and I told him there were some things I wanted to share with him. Papa grabbed my hands and said, "Martha, everything you tell me is safe. It won't ever leave this building."

I took a deep breath and began to verbally vomit all of my truths. Papa was the first person in my life that I had ever become completely honest with. As I poured my heart out, I remember feeling this huge burden being lifted from my being! I didn't have to lie to Papa anymore! It was so freeing! Papa knew in his heart most of the things I owned up to; as he had put most of the pieces together over the years and he was just waiting for me to feel comfortable enough to tell him. During that conversation, he said he knew that my current situation was not God's plan for me for my life and that he would do anything in his power to help me, but that he wouldn't rush into anything without the Lord's instruction. The instruction came in December of 2004.

CHAPTER 7

The Escape

On a miserably cold Wisconsin winter day, I called Smyrna as I had done many times before. But this phone call was different. She gave me the news that would change the trajectory of my life forever. Smyrna said, "Martha, I have to tell you something." She seemed hesitant and her voice quivered a little as she said, "I'm pregnant." I started screaming and jumping up and down. I was ecstatic! I knew in that instant that I had to escape and go be with her. After all, she had no one because she had separated herself from the group and married a heathen man. I purposed when I hung up the phone that day, come hell or high water, I would escape! I was not going to let my niece or nephew grow up without knowing me. I had grown up without my aunts and uncles and I was not going to allow this for the next generation. I didn't know how or when, but I just knew in my bones that this was it and with each breath I felt strength and determination settling into my mind, body and spirit! I told Papa of my purpose the next morning, and he said that he would pray on it.

Papa showed up at the shop three days later. He came inside to greet me and bounced up the front stairs with a huge grin. "Martha, go look out the back window." When I looked out the window, I saw a small white car sitting in the parking space where he usually parked. I looked at him confused. Papa said, "Martha, that car is yours!" I squealed with excitement and anxiousness. I hugged him over and over and thanked him. He had bought me a $1000 used Dodge Neon. I couldn't believe that Papa had bought me an escape car! I had a car that I drove from the compound to the shop each day, but it was my mom's. But Papa had thought of everything! I was so naïve and clueless. All I was worried about was escaping from the compound without getting caught. Getting caught and brought back was just not an option this time. I hadn't begun thinking logistically about what I would do once I escaped. How would I get back to North Carolina? Once I knew I had an escape car, the idea of my escape became real and almost inevitable at least to me.

I called Smyrna to inform her that I was going to run away and come home to be with her. I think she half-heartedly believed me. I know she wanted to believe it, but she knew my situation and how difficult it was going to be, plus she knew of my previous failed attempt.

For the next few days, Papa and I hatched a plan and went over different scenarios and details to ensure that I would be successful. I slowly started to smuggle my things out of the compound and would give them to Papa so he could put them in the escape car. Each day we would go over the plan and pray.

From the time Smyrna told me she was pregnant to the time of my escape, it was only about ten days. During that time, I busied myself at the shop creating a manual of how to do everything that I did to run the business. I was very detailed with creating processes and inventory lists. I didn't want to leave the group in a bad situation. I was the only one who knew the internal runnings of that shop. I also had an extreme amount of fear and guilt about planning to run away. I felt that I was sinning against Cultman again and that he had done so much for me and now I was basically spitting in his face by running away. I constantly struggled with those thoughts and feelings, but each time I found myself coming to the same conclusion. I was not going to let Smyrna have her baby alone. Also, I came to the very heavy realization that I was stuck and my life was going nowhere. If I wanted to get married or have any sort of life, I had to go make it for myself. When these feelings and emotions became overwhelming, I would call Smyrna or talk to Papa and they would reassure me that I could do it and I deserved to have a life! It was true, I wasn't living. I was merely existing. Then the day came.

On December 27, 2004 (almost exactly five years after my first escape), I went to work like I always did but today was different. I knew that I was opening and closing this shop hopefully for the last time. Papa came to the store that day, and I remember it being a very melancholy day. We were both so excited but also sad and scared. Excited because we knew today was the day. Sad because we both knew we would not see each other daily anymore. If today went as planned, I would make it safely to North Carolina in just a week or so. We were scared because if I was caught, what would the repercussions be this time? We discussed and prayed nonstop about each detail of how the night would go. We reminisced about the last four years, and all that had transpired. I talked to Smyrna several times, making sure that we all agreed on the details and the plan. Smyrna had found me a safe house to go to immediately after escaping. I just needed to make it about 45 miles into Green Bay to that safe house. The safe house was with a woman who had left the cult several years prior who had also lived in the compound at the same time I did. Smyrna knew she would understand my situation and knew she would be more than happy to help. I remember Papa getting ready to leave the store that day and both of us sitting on the entrance stairs holding hands and Papa praying a very gripping prayer. He begged God for comfort and strength for me, and asked that if it was God's will that

I would make a successful escape that night. My mind started racing as he prayed. What if this wasn't God's will! Papa left me that day in tears. I think he was worried it would be the last time he would ever see me.

The appointed time came; it was around 1am. This was generally the time when the guards would surely be asleep. There were always two or three guards posted at the exit of the compound and you could not leave without driving by them. As luck would have it, it began snowing very hard about 11pm and continued throughout the night. The guards slept soundly in their cars, as the snow piled up on their windshields. It was pointless to run their wipers as the snow was coming down too fast.

I loaded the last of my belongings from the compound into my mom's car as the snow was deepening. Then I got into the car, said a quick prayer, and started the car. Because of the amount of snow that had fallen, my tires spun as I tried to get traction. Fear gripped me, and my head began to pound. I just kept praying and gripped the steering wheel. Suddenly the car began to creep forward as it gained traction on the newly fallen snow. I was terribly afraid one of the guards would wake up and see me in my car struggling in the snow.

I pulled the car up to the gate that separated me from the compound and the outside world. I jumped out of the car and ran as quickly as I could to unhook the first chain and then the second. I jumped back in the car and pulled the car through. I could feel the fear enveloping my body as I reattached the top chain and then the bottom. I was less than a car's length from one of the guards. What if she heard me and woke up? It would all be over for me. I had come up with a cover story just in case, but I was hoping I would not have to use it.

My cover story was that I had to go down to the fudge shop because the alarm had been set off and I needed to reset it. This had happened in the past. I knew this was dangerous, though, because what if the guard followed me and realized the alarm wasn't going off. I would be caught in another lie.

I slipped out past the guards and through the gates undetected, and headed to Papa's house. He was standing in the window waiting for me. He rushed down the stairs to meet me at the door and hugged me so tightly! I don't think he really thought I would make it. We transferred all of my belongings quickly to the car he bought me and he followed me over to my mom's house to drop off her car, then he drove me back to his house. I knew I couldn't use my mom's car to escape because they would notify the police and say I had stolen the car since it was not in my name and they could possibly track me down that way. I couldn't risk it and that is why Papa had bought me a getaway car.

When we got to my mom's apartment, I used the emergency key she had given me, and slowly and quietly opened the door. I knew my mom was a very light sleeper and I could not take the chance of waking her, but there was a part of me that just wanted to see her in case this was the last time. I knew this thought was morbid, but it was a possibility because when you left the cult you were excommunicated and I knew my mom would not be allowed to see or talk to me again as long as she was part of the cult.

I laid her keys on the table with a letter to her and my baby brother. The two bedroom apartment was small, and I could see that both of the bedroom doors were cracked open. I quickly peeked in at Zeke, my youngest sibling, and then swiftly made my way to my mom's bedroom door and took a quick peek at her and then I slipped back out of the door just as quietly and quickly as I had entered. The letter I left was a goodbye letter. It told her that I had decided that I couldn't live this way anymore, and that I hoped I would see her again in the future and that I loved her and Zeke very much. I ran down the apartment stairs to Papa's car. I jumped in and we rode in silence back to his house. It was like we both knew the gravity of the situation and neither wanted to jinx it or talk about it. Plus we knew we only had minutes before they may be looking for me. If one of the guards woke up and noticed my car gone, the notifications would go out in a hurry and they would be after me.

Leaving Papa that night was one of the hardest things I had ever done! I knew that if I was caught that I would never be allowed to see him again, and if I made it back to North Caroline, I would not see him very often. Papa had been so good to me, and we had grown such an insanely deep connection for one another that it was extremely painful to say goodbye. Papa and I stood in his garage and he hugged me tightly as he prayed a loud and boisterous prayer that Jesus would protect me and guide my life for his glory, and on and on!

When we were done praying, he gave me an envelope with $1500 and a credit card. I hadn't even thought about having no money, I just wanted to be free, I was so naive! But Papa had truly thought of everything.

With another hug and prayer, I got in my car and my guardian angel watched me slip away into the night. The snow made it a very slow, scary and treacherous trip to the safe house, but on one hand I knew that even if they were looking for me, they weren't going anywhere very fast either. I made it to the main highway which is then a straight shot to Green Bay, and ever so carefully creeped my way towards safety. There were times when I could barely see three feet in front of me because of the blowing snow. It had pretty much stopped snowing by the time I reached the highway, but the wind had picked up and was making it very difficult to navigate. Then another small miracle occurred. A snowplow came up quickly from behind me and passed me. I quickly moved into his clearing and suddenly I was moving! I remember the only thought I had during that drive to the safe house was that my success will be my revenge. I repeated this over and over in my head. My success will be my revenge!

I got to the safe house and Leah greeted me with hugs and delightful shrieks! She could not believe I had made it. We stayed up all night catching up and talking. She reassured me that I had made the right decision and from what I could tell she was doing pretty well on the outside which was also comforting. I spent a couple of days hiding out with Leah. I knew that Cultman would have his henchmen out looking for me, so I needed to keep a low profile. I also didn't head back to North Carolina right away because I knew that would be the first place Cultman would send his henchman to look for me. I knew that I had to wait until things died down before I could make the trek back to North Carolina. Smyrna was the only one who knew of my plans and I knew that even if Cultman or anyone else tried to corner her, she would claim that she knew nothing.

I brought in the New Year with Leah and her husband. I remember celebrating that night and talking about all my hopes and dreams of my new life that I was embarking on. I was full of life and so excited for whatever life had in store for me, as long as it meant I was free! During those first few days of freedom, I tried to do things to help me fit in better with the outside world and look and feel less like I had just run away from a cult. I used some of the money Papa had given me to cut my hair, buy some new clothes (pants of course), and I bought my first cell phone.

PART 2

Growing Up Culty

CHAPTER 8

Home Sweet Home-ish

On January 3, 2005, I said goodbye to Leah and her husband and began the journey back to North Carolina. As I started the 20-hour drive, the reality of my freedom began to settle in my consciousness. Up until that point, I think I had been running on adrenaline and hope. It had now been nearly a week since I had escaped and I was more determined than ever that there was no way I was going back…EVER!

The drive was long, and I remember filling those hours by calling people. I talked to Smyrna, Papa, and some friends from high school I hadn't spoken to in over eight years. I remember the elation but also awkwardness of those phone calls to my friends who hadn't seen or heard from me in nearly eight years. To them, I had just poofed, disappeared. No one knew where I had gone after high school graduation. I would come to find out that the rumor mill had swirled many scenarios, from drug rehab, teen pregnancy, and even suicide, but no one suspected I was being held in the basement of a compound in a religious cult.

I remember calling Stacy Rae, one of my best friends from high school. She couldn't believe I was calling. She had so many questions! I remember telling her I had a lot of explaining to do, but I was just excited to be moving back to North Carolina and couldn't wait to see her! With each phone call, I felt more and more excited about the possibilities of a future outside of the cult! I was FREE; it was REAL!!! I had been successful!

The most important call I made was to my middle school best friend with whom I had not spoken to since the day before I had left North Carolina to return to the compound. I had no idea where she was or how to get ahold of her, but I remembered her home phone number from when we were kids and gave it a try. I remember the surprise in her dad's voice when I told him who it was. He said Shanna would be so excited to hear from me! He gave me her new phone number and told me I better come see him sometime; it's been way too long!

Shanna and I met when I was 12 years old in the 6th grade. We rode the same school bus. She was my first real friendship and she was my constant. We made so many memories and shared so many shenanigans. She was my best friend, but not even she knew my secrets. I disappeared from her, just like I had everyone else. I saw her the day before I left to return to the compound, but never told her of being summoned by Cultman. I just couldn't. She wouldn't understand.

I remember my heart beating as the phone rang and I waited for her to answer. She answered and when I told her it was me she said, "No way!" Screaming and yelling "MARV" ensued. Once she believed me and calmed down, I remember telling her I was on my way back to North Carolina and I needed somewhere to stay until I could get back on my feet. She didn't hesitate for a single second and invited me to stay with her, literally no questions asked. We talked off and on throughout that trip trying to catch up for the last eight years and reliving the wonderful, scary, and sometimes humorous memories we shared from our middle school and high school days. Talking to Shanna and knowing now I had a safe place to stay gave me a sense of peace and reassurance that everything was going to be okay.

The trip at points was treacherous! Living in Wisconsin and Minnesota, I was very familiar with driving in snow, but then I hit an ice storm in Kentucky. This I was not familiar with. Ice and mountain driving in the dark does not mix. I pulled off the highway and decided to stay the night at a small, rinky dink motel. I walked in the front door of the motel, and an old man of Indian descent looked up at me over the top of his glasses with a cigarette hanging from the corner of his lips and said, "Can I help you?" I said, "I am just looking for somewhere to get out of the weather. What is your cheapest room for one night?" He got me registered for a single room with a double bed for $31.00 for one night. I paid, he gave me the key, and I walked to my room.

I opened the door and stared almost in disbelief. The room was very old and worn. It appeared as if it had not had a face lift or a fresh coat of paint since at least the '70s. The comforter covering the bed was ratty and had cigarette burns in it. In front of the bed on a small dresser was a 13-inch TV with rabbit ears. The bathroom was dingy, cold and left something to be desired when it came to cleanliness. But all in all, the room was at least warm and safe from the wicked weather, and who was I to complain after all, just a week before I was sleeping on a concrete floor in a sleeping bag and walking a quarter of a mile to use the bathroom.

I didn't sleep well that night partially because of my anxiousness to get back to North Carolina safely, and partially because the wind was howling and the ice was slamming against the window panes as if someone was trying desperately to break into my room, which would have been a difficult feat because there were about six different deadbolts and latches on the door.

I woke up early the next morning and got back on the road. The roads were not great, but I white-knuckled it for hours until I was safely through the mountains. I remember the sun breaking through the clouds that morning and having this overwhelming feeling of excitement and gratitude. Excitement for a new chance at a brand new life. Gratitude for my safety, for Leah and the safe house, for Smyrna and my niece or nephew she was carrying, for Stacy Rae, and that I was getting closer and closer to Shanna's house.

I remember calling Shanna as I got close to Chapel Hill and telling her my estimated time of arrival. I know she couldn't help it, but she seemed skeptical that I was actually on my way and that I was going to actually show up. As I pulled onto her road, I will always have imprinted in my memory the smiling face of my best friend and her young three-year-old son standing at the mailboxes in their pajamas and slippers. I slammed the car into park when I saw her and ran to her with arms flailing and tears running down both of our faces as we both shrieked with delight! We embraced and looked up and down at each other as if in disbelief that we were in each other's presence.

I got back in the car and followed them up to their house. Shanna and I stayed up all night laughing and crying and just enjoying each other's company. One thing I will always be thankful for is that Shanna never probed for information about where I had been, what I had been doing, and why I was coming back. She was just so happy to have me back in her life and she didn't care who, what, where, when or why. Immediately we resumed a friendship as if I had never left.

I was safely in North Carolina for one day and I began to feel anxious. I needed to find a job; I needed to be busy to keep my mind from creating the worst-case scenario. Would I get caught, would I be strong enough if I did to stand up to them and refuse to be returned? Would that really work? Would all of this be in vain? What would my punishment be when I returned to the compound? These questions swirled around in my head like a cyclone constantly making me crazy and causing intense anxiety and anxiousness.

As luck would have it, I was able to get the first job I applied for which was a wait staff position at Carolina Meadows, a prestigious retirement community where I had also worked as a teenager. I remember being so excited that I was going to be paid $7.25 per hour! I hadn't been paid a red cent for close to five years! I was ready to get my life back plus I wanted to pay Papa back as quickly as I could. I worked a lot, picked up extra shifts when I could, and hung out with Shanna and her family during the rest of my free time.

I slowly began to open up to Shanna about where I had disappeared to for the last eight years. She always listened, held me and cried with me, but never judged. She just held space for me to share as I was ready, never pressing me for more than I was ready to share.

When I finally felt like enough time had passed, I went to see Smyrna but was constantly looking over my shoulder until I got there safely. I had to keep a low profile for quite a while because I knew that Cultman had people trying to track me down. Members could leave the cult on their own accord, but it was different for me. I had been "chosen," I lived in the compound and I knew too much. It was dangerous to allow me to be on the outside with all that I had experienced and seen at the hands of Cultman. Hence why I was hunted. Smyrna told me they had been to her house, and to my dad's and had also questioned my brothers. Once I was told that the hunt had died down I reconnected with three of my younger brothers. I will always remember the first time I saw my brother Reuben. Reuben and I had been very close growing up. He was the male version of me. He was the black sheep, the misfit and the one that constantly pushed boundaries. Reuben came to Shanna's house when he heard I was in town. I hadn't seen Reuben in well over six years. He had changed so much! I remember looking at him and wondering what happened to my little brother. He was now a man with facial hair and a deep voice.

I reconnected with Levi and Timothy shortly after that. They too had changed. The last time I had seen both of them was before they had run away from the cult. They didn't live in the compound, but they still had to run away to make a break from the group and from my mom. We all started hanging out and getting to know one another again. It was weird. We were siblings but knew very little about each other. In retrospect, a lot of life had been lived since we all had been together. They had created lives outside of the cult and were doing their best to navigate this crazy thing called life. Then I showed up trying to reconnect and bond with them, but I think mostly they perceived this as butting into their lives. It was tough. Although I was older, they were all far more mature and acclimated to the outside world than I was. Thus the reason I spent the first year or so after my escape, training in the school of hard knocks.

One of my first memories of my siblings' post escape was when my brothers and sister got together with Shanna and threw me a surprise birthday party for my 26th birthday at Chuck E Cheese! It was amazing! I had never ever celebrated a birthday before, and of course I had never had a party! My brother Levi was a manager there, so I got the VIP treatment. They went all out for ME. I was so blown away by their efforts that I didn't even realize that it was a kids' place and I was probably the first person over the age of 12 to celebrate their birthday at Chuck E Cheese, but I could not have cared less. That memory will forever be one of my favorites, because my siblings worked together to make my first birthday out of the cult so special. I hid out at Shanna's and kept a low profile for a couple of months. After my birthday party and reuniting with my brothers, I made the decision that I was ready to seek out my dad.

Cultman had instructed my parents to separate about five or six years before, so my father was living in North Carolina while my mother lived in Wisconsin not far from the compound. I know you are wondering, how in the world did Cultman separate your parents? Cultman had called my parents and told my mom that she was in grave danger and that my brother Reuben would end up killing her if she stayed. Reuben had gotten involved with drugs and the rave scene and knew no limits. Cultman preyed on this and instilled fear in my mom. She was told that for her safety and the safety of my younger brothers that they needed to move to Wisconsin right away. So, that is what they did. My dad stayed in North Carolina with Reuben and his business, and mom and my brothers moved to the compound. I was ecstatic to have family in the compound with me! But that only lasted a few weeks and my mom then got an apartment about 30 minutes away. Eventually, she ended up moving to an apartment about 10 minutes from the compound after Levi and Timothy had run away. My brother gave me an address, and I summoned all my courage and drove over to meet my dad.

I was extremely nervous and I had no idea what to expect, but I felt that sitting down with my dad was important. I didn't realize just how important it would be for the future of my family. I knocked on the door of dad's apartment. He came to the door shirtless, noticed it was me and scowled, "How could you do it, Martha? How could you leave after everything Cultman has done for you?," Dad asked. "I am ashamed of you, you need to leave, I have nothing else to say to you!," he blurted as he began to shut the door in my face.

As the door was being closed in my face, I knew this was my only chance. I pushed back on the door and I just stood there staring at my dad, tears welling up in my eyes, anger and sadness growing with each second. "Dad, please! I need five minutes of your time, please!," I stammered! He looked at me, his spirit clearly vexed, "Come in."

Over the next three hours, I detailed the last eight years of my experience in the compound. Mostly, my dad sat in silence and he let me speak. I cried and cried as I unloaded onto my dad all of the trauma that I had endured at the hands of Cultman. At the end of our conversation, my dad looked straight at me and said, "Martha, we had no idea. This is not what me and your mom signed up for when we joined the group. We thought you were in good hands! In our minds, there was no better place for you than with Cultman."

All these years later, I am grateful that my dad believed me. I did not have a great track record with him when it came to truthfulness and it had been many years since my dad and I had any type of conversation so he really had no reason to believe me. Many years later I asked him why he believed me that night. He said, "You were a good liar, but you weren't capable of making up the things that Cultman did to you." My conversation with my dad that evening would end up being the catalyst that began the process of my parents making the choice to separate themselves from the cult and begin their journey of healing and the rebuilding of our family.

I lived at Shanna's for three months until I had saved up enough money to get my own place. I called Papa almost daily. He was such an intricate part of my life, and I felt that I really owed my freedom to him. We ended every conversation with Papa saying a prayer for me. Papa continued to be my safe place, my refuge, and I enjoyed every phone call. I couldn't wait until the time when I would feel safe enough to go back up to Wisconsin to visit him.

I got my own apartment in March of 2005 and it was a huge deal. I had never lived by myself and had this type of independence. It didn't take long for my life to begin to spiral out of control. I was like a caged animal that had been set free, except I didn't know how to act responsibly with this amount of freedom. I began trying to make up for all the time I had missed by being in the compound. I began drinking excessively, smoking weed and sleeping with just about any man that paid me a little bit of attention. I had zero self-confidence, self awareness, self-worth and frankly I didn't like or value anything about myself. The lack of these things made for a dangerous concoction of life lessons and a lot of animalistic behaviors.

With that being said, and no matter how irresponsible my life choices were at that time, I never missed a day of work. I was committed to my job, and was quickly promoted. Part of that may have been because I was having inappropriate relations with the cook and my boss, both of which I am not proud of. I was a hard worker, so I chose to believe that since I was told by my superiors that my work ethic was second to none, that was the main reason promotions came and doors opened for me.

Within a couple of months, I took a job in patient care in the assisted living wing at Carolina Meadows. I loved one-on-one care and I was a natural. I only survived about one year at that before I realized I was not cut out for nursing. I could not handle my patients dying! I would become close to them and learn about their families and their pasts and then one day I would come to work and they would be gone. It was heart-wrenching. I have come to understand that because of my past I took each death personally like someone else that I cared about was abandoning me. In my past, nothing good ever lasted. It always went away or was taken away.

CHAPTER 9

Whirlwind Romance

On March 10, 2006, while still working at Carolina Meadows, the cosmos all came together and agreed that I had lost complete control of my personal life all the while thriving in my professional life and decided to shake things up a little bit.

I was actively dating a guy in jail. He was a guy I knew from middle school, and we reunited at a stop light as 26-year-old adults. Our eyes met and we recognized one another. We both pulled over into the Shell gas station, talked, and exchanged numbers. He was a good looking, dark skinned bad boy and he didn't try to hide it; to me it was part of his charm. We began dating, but from the beginning it was one-sided. I gave and he took. I allowed this because I had no self-worth, my moral compass was broken, and my self-confidence was non-existent. I heard rumors of him cheating and his scheming, but in my head what we had was different.

Not long after we began dating, he went to jail for possession of a controlled substance with intent to distribute. But lucky for us, he got work release weekly which meant that I could go get him and rent a motel room for a couple of hours and have nonstop sex. I'd like to say that this didn't feel good to me, and that I felt used and wanted better for myself, but that would not be true. I made up every excuse to make this situation okay, regardless of his demeaning behavior towards me. Looking back, I was stuck on our physical connection; I craved attention and intimacy!

My body had been abused and used before, so this was a disturbingly comfortable feeling. I also liked the feeling of being needed. I would give him money. Almost every time I went up to see him he needed money for a lawyer or this and that and the other. It was always something. Looking back, I am clueless how any of this seemed logical or worthwhile, but what I know to be true is that I was so desperate for attention that I didn't care what shape it took or how demoralizing it was to me. Inside, I was vacant, and I was constantly trying to fill that aching void.

On this particular day, I received a call from my brother's girlfriend's friend. Her name was Summer. She told me that her friend was out with my brother and she was bored. She pleaded with me to meet up after my shift for a drink at Bailey's, a local bar across from the hotel she was staying at. I declined at first because I was in the middle of my shift and by the time my shift would conclude I would have worked a double which is a 16-hour day. She continued to beg and I finally caved in and agreed. She had also mentioned that there was a cute guy at the front desk of the hotel and she thought she might invite him as well.

I arrived at Bailey's about 11:30 pm and immediately began pounding back the shots and chain smoking. Then Summer said, "Hey, look, it's him!" I looked over to see a handsome olive skinned guy, with dark black hair and a medium build walking towards our table. He greeted Summer and then looked at me and said, "Hi, I'm Samy," as he stuck his hand out for me to shake. I told him my name and he pulled up a seat. At that moment, I didn't realize those three words would completely change my life.

We spent the next couple of hours eating, drinking, and laughing. Samy was so funny, and he couldn't keep his eyes off me. I was smitten! Within 30 minutes or so we were feeding each other mozzarella sticks as we were getting to know one another. My recollections are foggy because of the amount of imbibing that I did that night, but I know that I kissed him several times before the bar closed at 2am. I also invited him to come back to my place, which was only about two miles from the bar.

At the time, I shared a duplex with my brother Levi which was a step up from the apartment that I lived in after moving out of Shanna's. He agreed to my proposal and we went back to my place once we ditched Summer back at the hotel. We continued kissing, talking and laughing all night. Neither of us barely slept a wink before it was time to get back up and go back to work. We exchanged numbers as he was leaving and he told me, "Last night was a lot of fun!" With a quick kiss on the lips and then the forehead, he rushed out the door and I hurried to get ready for work.

I remember that whole day so fondly. I floated around to my residence rooms as if I was on a big, fluffy cloud surrounded by rainbows and butterflies. I couldn't stop thinking about this guy, and how happy he made me, and how much we laughed! It felt so good to laugh! I was so giddy inside but reality would hit in between these wonderful thoughts. Will he call me? Was that just a one night stand? Damn, he's so cute! What does he see in me? While sitting on my lunch break, my cell phone rang and it was Samy! He said that he couldn't stop thinking about me and did I want to get together again that night. I tried not to act too excited about his invitation, instead I said, "Yes, that would be nice." Inside I was jumping up and down and screaming with excitement! These feelings were so unfamiliar to me, but I loved and was extremely freaked out by the way they made me feel!

We met back up that night at the same bar. I will never forget the anticipation I felt when I saw him pull into the parking lot. He was about 20 car lengths away from me when I saw him and I began running full speed towards him. As I approached, he opened his arms and I observed him smiling so hugely it made my heart leap with utter elation. I jumped into his arms and wrapped my legs tightly around his waist as I dug my face into his shoulder. He held me in his strong embrace for a few seconds before letting me down to the ground and stealing a kiss.

We walked into the bar hand in hand, my heart overflowing with excitement and wonder. We spent another night drinking, smoking, talking and laughing before heading back to my place for the night. Those two nights were the beginning and the ending for my life as I knew it. Samy and I slept in the next morning because neither of us had to work.

When I finally awoke, I looked at my cell phone to find over 30 missed calls and 20 some text messages. The majority of them were from my imprisoned boyfriend. CRAP, I had an imprisoned boyfriend! I had slept through our visitation hours and he was mad.

The last two days of bliss came to a sudden halt when I remembered I indeed had an imprisoned boyfriend. My heart raced and fear set in. His voicemails were threatening and angry and I knew that I would eventually have to answer his call.

The next time he called, I promptly told him matter of factly that this relationship was over and to please not call me again. My memory of that conversation has faded, but a few months later he showed up at my house and rang the doorbell. Samy received him and quickly let him know that he and I were together and it would be best if he left the property. That was the last time I heard from him; for at least 18 years.

On June 24, 2006, three and a half months after I met Samy, we married. Papa made the trip for our wedding in order to meet this man that had so quickly stolen my heart! From the moment I met Samy, I knew something was different, and I would tell Papa so. Papa was just so happy for me! It was not lost on me that the only reason I was getting a chance at love and marriage was because Papa trusted the Lord and reached out to save a lost soul…me! For a moment, I felt loved, safe and content.

Samy was a family-oriented, great guy, hard worker, and he loved me very much! Early on in our relationship, I had been open with Samy about my trauma filled past. He had reacted like anyone would have who heard that things of this caliber had happened to someone they loved. He was angry, sad and vowed he would go blow up the place if he could.

By the time I got married, my family was actively trying to rebuild. Smyrna had given birth to my niece Miliah the previous year and I was a very proud and involved auntie. Miliah was my 'reason.' I still tell her that to this day. I wanted to know her and love her so badly that it gave me the courage and motivation to reclaim my life outside of the cult. Now, my parents plus seven of the nine kids were out of the cult and we were all navigating the best we knew how. For some, that meant drugs and alcohol, for others that meant putting their heads in the sand and just taking it day by day and for me that meant striving for professional excellence all while keeping everyone at arm's length.

Acclimating to married life was hard. Samy was from a big family, and unbeknownst to me his mother moved in with us as soon as we got our own place. This was never a conversation that we had or discussed prior; it just happened. This added challenges to our new marriage. But what was even more challenging was that I had stopped running for the first time in almost 20+ years. You think this would be a good thing, but my nervous system didn't know what to do with this new experience. I created chaos in my marriage just to have something to freak out about. I got absorbed into my brother's drug-induced drama and bad situations because I was more comfortable being in fight or flight than I was being safe, loved and protected.

For years, I had a recurring subconscious nightmare. It wasn't when I was asleep; it chased me around all day. I used to think that I was going to wake up sometime and I would still be in the dingy corner of the compound basement, waiting for the days to turn into night so sleep would temporarily take me away from my reality. In the cult, sleep had always been my refuge. That was when I could shut out the world and retreat to my innermost self, where it was safe, where I wasn't scared of hearing Cultman's feet walking towards me. In the cult, when I was awake, I felt invisible, and useless unless I was being disciplined.

Samy was my rock! He was the only one who knew all of my secrets. Not even my family or Papa knew as much as Samy did, and he was still so kind, patient, and supportive. This new life seemed too surreal. It couldn't be real, and if it was, it wouldn't last. I was constantly waiting for the other shoe to drop, and Cultman's demeaning words would constantly circulate in my head, "You will amount to nothing and you will marry a nigger that beats you." I would tell Samy of my fears, and he would do his best to reassure me that if anyone ever came and tried to kidnap me and take me back to the cult that they would have to deal with him, there would be body bags involved and the bags wouldn't be for me.

Until Samy, I had never known what it felt like to be truly loved, cared for, worried about or felt understood. But simultaneously my insecurities, overactive emotional brain and fried nervous system made it very difficult for him in those early years of marriage. To further complicate things, I was so unhappy with myself, so damaged, and hurt that I turned and inflicted my brokenness on the one person that had never hurt me, abandoned me or betrayed me: Samy. Hurt people, hurt people.

I recognized my adverse behaviors and knew how I felt, but didn't know how to fix it. I went into survival mode. I began carefully constructing walls and barricades around my heart, my past and my trauma. Each day, I plastered on a smile and pushed through with fake positivity. In reality, I had so much to be grateful for! A loving husband, a beautiful home, a successful career, friends and family, but everyday I felt like a fraud and an imposter in my own life. I was consumed with making sure that no one knew of my past, my pain, and my secrets. I created an identity separate from the trauma and all my brokenness. I worked endlessly trying to overcompensate professionally and personally in attempts to keep others at bay, so scared someone might discover the real me. I became extremely successful in my job, but with all of the success, I was still empty, scared and imprisoned by my past. I was a shell of a person, trying to survive in a world I didn't fit in, and that I was constantly hiding from. Samy was present for me as much as he could be, or as much as I allowed him to be.

In April of 2010, I went into the hospital for a routine breast reduction. What ensued over the next six months was nothing short of dramatic. I contracted a strand of Methicillin-resistant Staphylococcus aureus (also known as MRSA) from the hospital that was resistant to antibiotics, and it took nearly ten days for my surgeon to diagnose this correctly. In the meantime, my breast flesh was being eaten alive, minute by minute. Each day the open wounds on my breast grew larger and began to open up under my armpits as well. When the diagnosis finally came, I was immediately brought back to surgery to have my wounds cleaned and debrided. Then my wounds were stuffed with silver sponges and I was wrapped tightly with what looked like saran wrap and hooked up to a vac pump. The wrapping and vac pump kept oxygen from getting to the wounds and slowly the wounds began to heal.

I was on the pump for eight weeks. During that time, I went into the hospital every three or four days to have the wrapping and sponges removed and then rewrapped with clean ones. Once the vac pump had done all it could do for my healing, I started having reconstructive surgeries. I was cut hip to hip in order to retrieve fat deposits that were implanted into my breast cavities. I ended up with multiple surgeries and endless skin grafts during the reconstruction process. I was out of work for nearly six months. This experience was as traumatic as it sounds, but Samy continued to be my support system! He took family medical leave and stayed with me for weeks, giving me medication, helping me eat, and using the bathroom as I had no upper body strength. He slept on the floor for months because he was scared of accidentally hitting me in his sleep or getting tangled in my vac pump or drain tubes and wires. Once I was released and able to go back to work, I did what I did best. Buried myself in my work! I jumped back in and engrossed myself with anything and everything that would grow my career and keep attention off of what was really going on with me internally.

It didn't take long before it seemed that this last traumatic event had put my nervous system over the edge. The outward manifestations of my traumatic past were now rearing their heads in every way possible. The complete unraveling of my life began, and I started to realize the cloak I had been dragging around, and the fortress of protection I had built from my past was no longer sustainable. I had become painfully overweight at 274 pounds, had major gastrointestinal issues, hormonal imbalance, chronic back and neck pain, migraines, allergy flare-ups and had just become extremely physically unhealthy! I was plagued with nightmares, walking in my sleep, sleep talking/screaming, anxiety, panic attacks, fear causing erratic behavior (like peeing in clothes baskets). All of these things that were happening to me was an outward manifestation of an internal problem, but it would be many, many, many years before I understood that. But what I did know and understand was I just couldn't deal with myself, with the pain, anxiety or my crazy and invading catastrophic thoughts any longer!

I had a bad habit of running every time that things got tough in my marriage. Samy was so patient and understanding at first but finally in a loving but personal way he had to put his foot down and drew a very clear line in the sand. One night after a fight I ran out the door, slamming it behind me and got in my car and left for hours. Samy of course was worried and upset and when I returned he let me know that if I left again in that manner that our marriage would be over. That was the last time I ran, at least in that manner. Every time we fought or we had a disagreement and I ran, I was running from myself! I was convinced that he would quit on me so I wanted to quit first! I now understand that I was just a scared little girl who had been running since age eight or nine, and didn't have the mindful comprehension or tools to know how to handle her pain and emotions differently. Samy putting up this boundary got my attention. I needed help! But from where? From whom?

I looked up a local therapist and attended three sessions. Each session was pretty much spent crying and blowing my nose. Every time she asked me a question, I would start to answer and then would become consumed with emotion. At the beginning of my fourth session, my therapist said, "Martha, I am really sorry, but I have never treated anyone from a cult, so I do not feel like this is a good fit and it is outside my scope of practice." She apologized that she didn't know of anyone in particular to refer me to, and wished me good luck. I left her office devastated! I was too broken for even a professional! This event hurled me further into the depths of pain, despair, nightmares, and anxiety. No one would be able to understand me or help me. I felt so alone, so worthless, so sad, and in so much pain, yet, I remembered the words I told myself the night I escaped, "My success will be my revenge!" I couldn't give up!

I made the decision to go to my primary care doctor and asked for some help. I beat around the bush and didn't dare allow her to get too close to my trauma, but I was honest when I told her I was struggling. I explained my anxiety, that I found myself crying all the time, and about all of my physical woes. She prescribed me Prozac, and then gave me several referrals to specialists.

Leaving the office that day, I felt a glimmer of hope. My doctor had at least listened to me, and given me somewhere to start to address all that was going on with me. She referred me to the ENT, a Gastroenterologist, a Spine and Orthopaedic doctor, and to a Neurologist. For the next several months, I bounced around the healthcare system from one specialist to another, hoping someone would help relieve this deep and nearly debilitating sadness and do something or give me something to numb the pain in my physical body on the outside and inside of me. My physical body ached tremendously every single day!

As I visited each specialist, I left feeling even more broken and overwhelmed as they bestowed upon me one diagnosis after another. I was diagnosed with fibromyalgia, migraines, post-traumatic stress disorder (PTSD), depression, anxiety, Polycystic ovary syndrome (PCOS), neuropathy, disc degeneration, and that's just a partial list of all the labels I received. No wonder I felt like shit! Each specialist I visited just treated my symptoms from the perspective of their specialty. None of them saw the full picture! The real me; a broken, abused, scared and traumatized little girl who just needed someone to hold her and tell her she was worthy of healing and in time it was all going to be okay!

My symptoms were absolutely a physical manifestation of my body keeping the score of all the trauma I had experienced in my life. My physical symptoms were part of an overloaded internal ecosystem that was shutting down one piece at a time. This pain was now so deep that it was on a cellular level. My mind, body and spirit could no longer support the walls, distractions, poisonous self-talk or anything else that was keeping me from addressing the core issue: my trauma. But how?

CHAPTER 10

Help!

I was a practicing Therapeutic Medical Massage Therapist as well as an Administrative Director for three Physical Therapy clinics and I had taken some continuing education classes that had discussed how trauma gets stored in your cells and muscles. Something clicked inside me! Yes! This made so much sense to me.

It was at this point that I decided to take my life back. I became my own advocate and started doing my own research. I began reading and taking classes about holistic and naturopathic ways to heal and deal with the kinds of symptoms I was experiencing.

I like Gladys McGarey's description of holistic medicine in her book *The Well-Lived Life*. "The term holistic medicine refers not to the strategy but to the approach. It's about treating the whole patient, not just the disease. It's about seeing each individual as a complete and complex being, one with a unique set of physical, psychological, and spiritual characteristics." YES, I needed this approach! I poured myself into learning about each modality and I committed myself to trying anything and everything at least once. If it didn't resonate, I moved on. I now understand that I was beginning to tune into my intuition. I found so many helpful modalities on my healing journey, and it seemed that when one had run its course the next thing I tried would peel yet another layer.

In pursuit of a healthier, happier, more whole me, I embraced many modalities, some mainstream or modern western medicines and others that were holistic or naturopathic. Some of those were talk therapy, cognitive therapy, eye movement desensitization and reprocessing (EMDR), biofeedback, neurofeedback, massage, chiropractic, cranio-sacral therapy, reiki, spiritual mentorship, breathwork, hypnosis, life/health coaching, myofascial release, acupuncture, and most importantly, I found my faith again! I could write at length about how each modality chipped away at my trauma and got me one step closer to who I was meant to be, but I am careful to share too much as everyone's experience is so drastically different, and in healing, one size does not fit all.

For me, my broken soul and spirit aching from incredible amounts of trauma inflicted on and settled in on a cellular level could not be healed with western medicine. There wasn't a prescription that could heal my wounds. They were too deeply wrapped around the spindle fibers of my very being. No pill could reach that space. I had to do the work of repairing and loving all of the wounds and scars that had been created by each traumatic action taken against me, each word that had been spoken to tear me down, and each assault that had been meant to keep me meek, humbled and small. It would be my responsibility to myself if healing was to be had.

Some modalities I shared above like EMDR, bio and neurofeedback, hypnosis, and cognitive therapy proved beneficial as a tool for going inward, and reconnecting with the broken, hurt, sad, lost and betrayed little girl: Martha Glory. Once that connection was made, then I started using other modalities to heal those hurts, betrayals and brokenness such as talk therapy, cranio-sacral therapy, reiki, spiritual mentorship, myofascial release and acupuncture. Lastly, I used and continue to use other modalities such as coaching, breathwork, massage, chiropractic, yoga, journaling and other mindfulness practices to step into my power and continue to grow in self-love and self-confidence and elevate on this healing path. This three-part healing journey has taken over a decade and I'm grateful to Debra, my Reiki instructor and Craniosacral practitioner, who started me on the path.

During this process, I experienced so many highs and lows. The dark night of the soul is a real thing! Both before I began my healing journey and during, I had been stuck in that night for a very long time. Faith had not played a part in my life, maybe ever at least in a personal way! Everything I knew about faith in a positive way was what I had learned from Papa. But Papa had not warned me how hard life would be on the outside! For years, I felt forsaken and abandoned by God. I was certain God was angry at me for my sins, and I had a lot of them!

That all changed one fall evening on a Thursday about four years into our marriage. Samy and I had a disagreement, and so I went for a run. Let me remind you, I had promised Samy I would never get in my car and run away from him again, but he never said I couldn't go for a run! When I say run, I mean a brisk walk, but nevertheless, I left on foot and with no particular destination in mind, I just needed to burn off some steam. I had found it useful to move my body and walk or run when I became overwhelmed, frustrated or anxious and this situation qualified as such so off I went. I went in a direction I had never gone before taking this sidewalk and then crossing a road and taking another sidewalk, and just going and going. I was in the zone, and completely preoccupied with feeling sorry for myself that I hadn't realized where I was going or that the sidewalk had ended. I stopped. I looked up and I realized I was in front of a building. There was a small marquee on the right side of the glass doors and it said "Do you know how much Jesus loves you?" I swallowed hard!

I didn't feel loveable. In fact, I felt unworthy of Samy's love, how could Jesus love me? He clearly didn't know how bad I was? I sat down on the bench outside those glass doors, put my face in my hands and wept. I don't know how long I sat there, but it was long enough for Jesus to sneak his way into my heart. Suddenly I stopped crying. I felt lighter. As I stood up from the bench, I looked back at the marquee. It said "Welcome to Grace Church, Welcome Home, We are Reaching People and Building Lives. Sunday: 10am Service." I took a deep breath, smiled and began to walk home. I made a mental note to go back to this building at 10am on Sunday, which was 2.5 days away. Samy was working 2nd shift at that time, so he came home and went to bed around 4am, and generally slept until early afternoon. On Sunday, I got up and went back to Grace Church. I sat in the back, and I remember crying throughout the entire service. The worship touched my soul in a way that the worship at the cult never had! Then the sermon began and it felt like Pastor Kendrick was speaking directly to me! Martha…. "God sees your pain, he knows your sins and he knows your heart and still he loves you. He died on the cross for you and for me!" OMG!!!! Papa's familiar words rang in my thoughts! Papa was right! This was such good news!!! Jesus knew my sins and still loved me! For the next couple of months, I went to Grace Church each Sunday at 10am. I stopped sitting in the back. I moved myself up to the second row right behind the pastor's family. Something was happening inside of me, and it felt amazing, and I wanted more of it. Slowly my walls started to come down regarding faith and I made the conscious decision to Go All In. This was the beginning of how I found my faith when I needed it the most.

As I continued to do the internal work that healing requires, I tapped into something spectacular and faith played a huge role in this discovery. I found ME! Under all the pain, trauma, labels, responsibilities, expectations, there she was! She was banged up, scarred, bruised, and scared but she was beautiful! She was me, "fearfully and wonderfully made in the image of God." That was a breakthrough! I began the journey of self-love, self-awareness, and began uncovering the Martha Glory who was worthy of love, grace and mercy. It was then that I realized I couldn't fully love myself if I didn't believe that I was first loved by God and secondly that I was "fearfully and wonderfully made" by God. And if I believed this about God, then I had no choice but to truly surrender and accept his grace, mercy and forgiveness completely. This decision was a game-changer! Faith became the pillar of my fortitude, courage, strength, resilience and my healing!

As I continued the inner work and healing of my past and trauma, I noticed my physical ailments started to dissipate as well. My nightmares began to turn to dreams where I was now in control of the situation instead of the terrifying nightmares I had been plagued with for many years previously. My depression and anxiety were under control and I was able to come off of Prozac within the first year of this journey. Seeing these interconnections kept me motivated to keep going, to continue to do the work, and to keep peeling the layers of pain back and exposing the next wound so that it could scab over and heal. Although these wounds left scars, I began to see how these scars would tell a story; they would be my testimony for the rest of my life. Those scars to this day stand for God's love, redemption, resilience, strength, worthiness, hope, forgiveness, wisdom and so much more that is still unfolding because my testimony is not finished.

As I continued this process, I became more and more intrigued by the depths of the links and connections of absolutely everything: mind, body and spirit. In the years ahead I would begin to study this so I could teach others.

I committed the next five years to getting healthy, body, mind and spirit! The outward results were drastic but nothing in comparison to what was happening on the inside. During this time, I became my biggest cheerleader, I pushed myself and found strength and fortitude

I didn't know that I possessed. I trained, participated and finished a woman's triathlon. I released almost 100 pounds and have kept most of it off for over a decade. My fibromyalgia disappeared, migraines lessened, back and neck pain improved drastically, gastrointestinal issues healed, allergies improved, my chronic pain issues that had been plaguing me for years slowly became a non-issue, but most importantly the heavy rock I had been carrying around in my head and chest for decades became smaller and smaller until it vanished. These results proved to me that again everything is connected! I realized quickly that the more I was aware of my nervous system and I learned how to regulate it, my physical and emotional body responded positively as well! How did I regulate my nervous system? There are many ways.

Some that worked well for me were taking a walk outside, finding opportunities to move my body through dance, freestyle jumping, swaying anything to keep my life force energy moving. Some of the other ways I helped my nervous system regulate were through 5x5x7 breathing, yoga, prayer, meditation, journaling and doing other acts of service and self-care. Acts of service such as volunteering is a wonderful way to calm your nervous system. Giving to others and giving back feels good and you feel useful. It helps put your pain in perspective and allows for a deeper understanding of your healing. The foundational principles that I learned through all the modalities that I worked through have continued to help me navigate the circumstances and trials that I have continued to experience on my journey.

All in all, these last 19 years since escaping the cult have been hard, exhausting, and debilitating at times, but it's also been enlightening, healing, and purpose-driven! I have reclaimed who I am and who I am meant to be! I realized I had to feel in order to heal, and I had to forgive, trust, surrender, and accept the flaws in others in order to truly find freedom from my past! I had to go inward.

CHAPTER 11

Messy Mess

So, what's my message in the mess? I have learned so many lessons on this amazing healing adventure, some enlightening and some terrifyingly painful, but all important! My lessons learned could alone fill up an entire book, but I will narrow it down and share some of the most impactful ones.

First, I am born complete and whole, and all that I am and need, God has already provided and put inside me; I just needed to uncover it, dust it off and clean it up so I could begin to shine. With this knowledge, I had to lovingly notice my healing journey from a place of curiosity, not judgment! I had to consciously build a completely new relationship with myself from the things I uncovered. I had to dismantle piece by piece all of the things I thought I was, was told I was and had unintentionally become in order to get to the gem of who God has called and created me to be. I AM different now after all of the trauma and my life experiences, and that's okay! Change is a must! Healing is a journey, not a destination.

I will never be able to say I am healed while I am in this human form, because life continues to happen which means the process of healing needs to continue as well. There have been and will be times when old mindsets, recurring patterns or limited beliefs creep in and wreak havoc on relationships, situations and have caused me to go into fight or flight! But, now I am able to quickly recognize this as a trigger, and I have found the courage to be able to recalibrate, set healthy boundaries, and navigate forward asking myself from a place of curiosity rather than judgment, does this serve me? If it doesn't, I am brave enough to let it go, take a different road, or make a choice more in alignment with who I am and what is important to me. After all, the only constant is: change.

Embracing change and being flexible allows for breakthroughs and new experiences. In my life, new opportunities and growth always came with making a change. Sometimes making a change is hard, painful, scary and fear creeps in trying to thwart your blessings and growth. In these moments, we have to "Do it afraid," to quote Joyce Meyer. In her book *Do it Afraid: Embracing Courage in the Face of Fear* she goes on to explain, "Freedom from fear doesn't mean the absence of its existence, but the refusal to let it control your decisions and actions." I have learned over and over that "Everything you want is on the other side of fear," ~Jack Canfield. Fear can be a healthy motivator if you allow it to, but there is a fine line because it can keep you stuck as well. I heard a powerful quote from an unknown source about a decade ago and it has stuck with me. "The brave man is not he who does not feel afraid, but he who conquers the fear." You just have to be willing to "do it afraid" and take the first step.

Next, our thoughts and the words we speak are more powerful than we can even comprehend. Your thoughts and beliefs create your worldview and future. If you say or think, "Today sucks!," guess what? You are probably going to have a crappy day. But if you reframe that and say, "Today has been challenging but I am up for it! Today is still going to be a great day!" Guess what? You will experience a great day even with the day's challenges. The fact is that you are indeed in control of your thoughts. Becoming the master and commander of your thoughts and beliefs is the most important work you will ever do when it comes to self-development, self-love and self-growth. Becoming keenly aware of your thoughts and having the ability and intentionality in redirecting, reframing and sharpening them will be a game changer!

Gautama Buddha says, "We are what we think. All that we are arises with our thoughts. With our thoughts, we make the world." Our thoughts have power! The words we speak are equally as powerful! I heard a preacher say some years ago, "You are either blessing or cursing yourself daily. Watch your words." That hit me in the gut!

I spoke horrible things to myself daily, things that I never dreamed of telling someone else! Dang, you are so fat! Nobody can love you, you are too broken. Everyone you love will eventually leave you. You will always be alone. You are lazy! You are ugly and defiled! And on and on!

When I realized with my words I was creating my worst reality, I decided, "Oh, heck no!" And at that very moment I stopped the self-betrayals and insults, I quit speaking unkindness and evil over myself and I began doing mirror work. In Louise Hay's book, *You Can Heal Your Life*, she talks about mirror work as a tool for self-acceptance and self-love. When I first started this work, it was very uncomfortable! It was so hard to look straight into the mirror and say something nice to myself. I would just get angry and cry. But I stuck to it! Within about a week or so, I was able to start saying things like, "Martha, I am so proud of you for not giving up!" "Martha, you are strong, and I am proud of you for showing up for yourself!" Eventually, those words seeded themselves deep in my psyche and heart! I began to only speak love, kindness, strength, gratitude, and abundance over myself.

When this new way of speaking to myself became a habit, I realized that I started speaking to others differently as well, to their face and behind their back. I made the conscious decision to only speak positivity, encouragement, kindness, and love over others as well and this decision has served me greatly. Becoming the master of my thoughts and the guardian of my words has been life giving!

A cool thing happened that I'd like to share. I was saying and thinking these positive things about myself, and then I realized I was actually feeling them and believing them as well! That was incredible. I felt like at first I had to be uncomfortable and kind of fake it till you make it, but the more consistently I treated myself in this positive and life giving way, the quicker it just became who I am! "Words are the most powerful thing in the universe....Words are containers. They contain faith, or fear, and they produce their kind." ~Charles Capp. So, simply said, change your thoughts, choose your words, change your life! I have come to live by the powerful motto, "The best is yet to come."

Another powerful lesson learned was that we cannot alter, fix or change the events of our past. All we can do is change our attitudes towards them. Every single moment is a choice and a gift. Once the moment passes, there are no redo's. We have to choose how we react, how we heal and how we move forward. Staying stuck is also a choice; every decision is a choice. I realized that my decision to heal was in actuality a profound gift to me and those around me. As I began to love myself and prioritize my healing, I became more capable of giving and sharing that love with my family, friends and others. My heart was becoming open again. Real healing happens on many levels, but the most important is on the heart level. God is love, and if I believe that to be true, then that must be my foundational principle as well.

It is my understanding that everything starts with God/Love and ends with God/Love. Love is one of the highest vibrations and love in itself is healing. Love dispels fear, because love is infinitely more powerful than fear. Most religions have love as a foundational principle. Why? Because love is the only thing that has the ability to sneak into and bring light to those places that have been abandoned, closed off, and left to die, those places that are most painful, shameful, fear filled and ugly, love is the only thing that heals all by bringing newness, renewal, aliveness, and a chance to try again.

Next, forgiveness! This was a difficult one to swallow. You want me to forgive those that have done horrible things to me? You want me to forgive myself? No way! I was angry at myself and others! Why had so many people done so many bad things to me? Why hadn't I been stronger, wiser or less trusting? The 'whys' will consume you and keep you stuck if you let them. You cannot be angry and have forgiveness at the same time. What I learned about anger is, "Anger is foolish, it eats at the soul." ~Brian Weiss, MD.

In order to truly be set free and heal from my past, I had to first let go of the anger and the whys and then forgive the perpetrators and those who had violated me. But before I could do that, I had to forgive myself! This was a tough process! I had to sit with myself in all my vulnerability and rawness and look into my own mind, body and spirit and forgive myself! This did not happen overnight; it was a painful uncovering but what I found beneath all of the lies, shortcomings, mistakes, heartache, and protective sheath was a brighter, lighter and more elevated piece of myself. In that noticing, I understood why forgiveness for self was so important.

I remember explaining forgiveness to Samy one night. He thought I was crazy! "Why would you ever consider forgiving them, Martha?" What I came to understand about forgiveness is that it was not for the perpetrators or violators, it was for me! I had never had the chance to tell any of the people that had hurt me in my past that I had forgiven them (until very recently). But because I had forgiven them in a deep and profound way, a huge rain cloud was lifted off of me and the sun began to sneak its way into the crevices of my soul and I slowly began to lighten up! One thing I have noticed about forgiveness: When you have truly forgiven someone or something, when you see that person, or hear their name or see something that reminds you of something painful, you do not have an emotional reaction. Your peace is in forgiveness.

In the process of writing this book, I shared a story of the man in jail that I dated right before I met Samy. Two days after typing those words into my manuscript, I received a Facebook request from that blast from the past. He sent me a private message and said he had been looking for me for many years and just wanted to apologize for the way he treated me and for putting me through things that I did not deserve. I was taken aback!

It was more than 18 years since I had even thought about that person, and I had forgiven and moved past that situation over 15 years ago! I responded to him via Facebook and explained that he owed me nothing, and that I had forgiven myself and him for that situation so many years ago. He was so happy to receive a response from me and we chatted briefly and he asked if I would call him when I had time. I did so that evening. We talked for about 30 minutes. He apologized over and over as we reminisced. I received his heartfelt apology and as we continued to talk I realized a piece of me was healing that I didn't even know was still hurting. This exchange was a divine gift and I received it.

I shared the serendipity of my current situation with him, how just days earlier I was writing about our brief dramatic and chaotic love affair. The next evening, I met him for drinks. So much time had passed, but so much time had stood still for him. He had spent nearly 13 years of the last 18 years in prison. He gazed at me almost star struck. "Martha, you look the same but totally different," he kept saying. I thought he was referring to my outward appearance. "No, it's something else." I told him that lots of people including my dad have told me that as I have healed I look lighter and more radiant. He agreed emphatically, "Yes, that is what I'm trying to tell you!"

As our conversation continued, I could not help but think how time had changed him for the better. He was gentle, kind and so vulnerable. He was becoming the man he was meant to be. So many years ago, I had seen a rougher, harder, less refined side of him, and now I looked at him with pride. He was doing the work to tap into who God had created him to be. Before we parted, I shared with him how touched I was that after all these years he had the courage to contact me and to ask for forgiveness and closure for a wound created almost two decades prior healing another piece of my brokenness, and I was grateful.

Another important lesson that I have learned and that has become an everyday practice for me is gratitude. Gratitude has been essential in my healing journey. True gratitude is a feeling, a connection, an action, and an emotion, but most importantly it's perspective. Gratitude is also a choice. I made the choice to live a healthier, happier life mind, body and spirit and as we have previously discussed, everything is connected. So in order to manifest that choice, I had to begin my healing journey.

Gratitude as a practice helped me to develop a more positive outlook on life, and it helped me look past my experiences and focus only for that moment on the present. I found that you cannot be truly grateful without being present. Some of the other benefits of gratitude are emotional regulation, reduced stress, improved cardiovascular health, improved mental health and mental clarity, just to name a few. The cultivation of a grateful mindset has been shown to boost happiness and life satisfaction.

Practicing gratitude also strengthened my interpersonal relationships. I learned to express appreciation more frequently, leading to better communication, trust, empathy and connections with family, friends, co-workers and even strangers. I found that gratitude used as a tool helped me to resolve conflicts and foster a more positive atmosphere in both my personal and professional settings. Through my gratitude practice, I have learned to reframe challenges and setbacks as opportunities for introspection and growth. By acknowledging and appreciating the lessons learned from difficult experiences, I have developed greater resilience and coping strategies, helping me navigate life's ups and downs with more ease and a positive mindset. I have adopted gratitude as a mental habit and I intentionally practiced it consistently until it just became part of who I am, and because of this, I find I am a healthier, happier, more adaptable, and more fulfilled individual.

I've also learned on this journey that just because I have constantly been seeking personal and professional development for over a decade and I am intentionally pursuing and doing things to promote self-growth, self-love and self-awareness, this will not keep life from happening. Shit will inevitably still hit the fan. What it does mean is that this work gives me the tools to navigate as life happens, to be able to ebb and flow allowing me to bounce back more quickly and with a lesson learned rather than beating myself up and sitting stuck in failure, disappointment, judgment or feelings of not being good enough.

This next one was brutal to have to learn, and I have unintentionally taken several painful opportunities to learn it. It is as follows. When you commit to being authentic and surrendering to your highest self and all that God has called you to be, you will be required to release, let go of and walk away from things, relationships, people, friends, feelings and situations because they no longer serve you or are not in alignment with who you are becoming. Everyone and everything cannot be part of your next season or future. Some things must be shed like a snake sheds its winter skin in order to make space for the new things that are in alignment to take its place.

During this season of releasing that which no longer served me, I left a good paying career in corporate to pursue my own gifts and passions. I had been doing Therapeutic Massage Therapy on the side for years, and I was gifted at it. So, I started PIC Wellness LLC and went all in. I loved the freedom that I found in just doing what I was passionate about rather than forcing myself to be in the corporate box where people are just numbers and the bottom line is more important than how we treat our employees. The reduction in my pay was significant, but the overall benefits physically, emotionally, and spiritually outweighed the financial discomfort. I made up the difference by nannying. I did not have children of my own, but I had always loved children and God had given me opportunities to help raise and nurture many.

Sometimes our highest good means walking away, or making painful changes in order to elevate us to where we are meant to be. In understanding this lesson, I made the heart-wrenching decision in October of 2020 to leave my almost 15-year marriage to Samy. Samy stood by me through my most difficult and painful healings and eventually it took a toll on our marriage. There were many other complicating factors on both sides, but I am accepting my portion. My healing and growth had taken priority instead of my marriage, and the result was our love story became stale. I was growing and changing and I came to the realization that I had outgrown my marriage.

After my separation and impending divorce, I needed to regroup. I needed time to just get away and really continue this deep inner work that I had been embracing. I took a two-year hiatus and moved to Virginia to help my best friend StacyRae build a retreat experience on the farm where she was living. This was an amazing season and the views were absolutely spectacular. The farm sits in the valley of the Blue Ridge Mountains and the 360 panoramic view is nothing short of God's artwork! I worked with and met incredible people, and learned so much about the animals, healing the land, and what it took to create an amazing retreat experience for the groups that we were honored to host and share with. I served as a sous chef for most of the events, to a young, incredibly talented up and coming chef, Jordan. This serene location and overall experience allowed me the space to further discover more about myself, my desires and capabilities. This whole experience was food for the mind, body and spirit! My cup was truly running over!

But, leaving my marriage had left a hole. I craved and yearned for the attention and love of a man. Five months after being in Virginia, I rushed into a new relationship with Stan. Within just five months of dating we got engaged and I moved off the farm and in with Stan. We lived remotely, to say the least, in central Virginia. The views of the mountains and rolling hills were breathtaking. Stan had built his dream house on 19 acres of beautiful wooded bliss in the middle of nowhere. It was peaceful, no neighbors, and the wildlife was thriving. Even in all of this beauty, I often felt lonely. I had no family, no friends and no community there. Stan worked long hours and that left me alone at home for most of the day.

I decided to go back to school and get my Life and Health Coaching Certification. I temporarily felt better in my situation because I had somewhere to focus my energy. I tried to convince myself that this life was everything that I thought I wanted and needed, but there was only one problem. I was still healing, growing, evolving and elevating and I once again outgrew the relationship. I lived with him for 15 months and we were planning our future when I realized that familiar feeling of complacency and inauthenticity. The relationship and rural living wasn't in line with who I was becoming, and once again with a heavy heart I had to walk away from love, stability, security and what I thought was going to be my future. Again, there were other complicating factors and red flags but my desire to be loved and appreciated painted them white and in the end we both ended up broken hearted.

Lastly, and arguably most importantly, I know who God says I am. I am faith filled, strong, courageous, powerful and worthy of a whole and complete joy filled life, and each day I wake with breath in my lungs is a gift and an opportunity to create just that! I will never again sacrifice myself to fit into someone else's box or dream. I will not and cannot shrink myself because of someone else's insecurities. I am light, and I am meant to shine! I am meant to share my truth and vulnerabilities with others so they feel comfortable to share theirs and thus find healing.

"Our deepest fear is not that we are inadequate. Our deepest fear is that we are powerful beyond measure. It is our light, not our darkness that most frightens us. We ask ourselves, 'Who am I to be brilliant, gorgeous, talented, fabulous?' Actually, who are you not to be? You are a child of God. Your playing small does not serve the world. There is nothing enlightened about shrinking so that other people won't feel insecure around you. We are all meant to shine, as children do. We were born to manifest the glory of God that is within us. It's not just in some of us; it's in everyone. And as we let our own light shine, we unconsciously give other people permission to do the same. As we are liberated from our own fear, our presence automatically liberates others." ~Marianne Williamson, A Return to Love: Reflections on the Principles of "A Course in Miracles"

The first time I read that, it resonated so deeply and I felt the words in my very core! I am a child of God! I will shine my light so it gives others permission to step into theirs! Over the years my faith has continued to evolve. My faith and my belief in God is personal and I feel fortunate to understand God's love for me. Psalm 18:2 *New International Version,* says "The LORD is my rock, my fortress and my deliverer; my God is my rock, in whom I take refuge, my shield and the horn of my salvation, my stronghold."

Over the last three years or so, I've made the purposeful decision to use my healing journey to help others turn their trauma into triumph and transformation. I am now a Certified Life and Health Coach, spiritual mentor, keynote and motivational speaker, and Best-Selling Author. Most importantly, I serve as a Life Visionary. I help those who are ready to intentionally peel off the layers of their past trauma, pain, failures, bad habits, and anything else that may be holding them back and help them to envision and step into their God-given gifts, talents and purpose. It's my passion to help others look inward to reclaim self! The ability to reclaim self is transformative! When you can clearly see who you are and who you were created to be, you become unstoppable! The vision becomes passion and the passion becomes purpose. It's my honor to help survivors to become warriors!

There is an amazing freedom that comes when you know you are truly living and working in your purpose and giftings, and the bonus is being able to share those with others! That's the season of life that I am in today. Everything that I have been through, experienced and healed from has brought me to this beautiful place where I am now able to be the advocate, resource and guide for others that are ready to stop just surviving and are ready to take back their lives, reclaim their power, and become a warrior!

I look forward to continuing to be a positive voice for the voiceless, and to be a beacon of light for those who struggle in the pain of darkness! My message to all struggling: You are never truly alone! You may feel lonely, but I am here to remind you, darkness is just the absence of light, it doesn't have to be permanent! We get to choose at every moment whether to stay stuck in our pain, or to reach out our hand and ask for help! You are worth that choice, choose you, choose your healing.

Not too many years ago, I had to humble myself and bare my shame, guilt, fear, brokenness and the ugliest parts of me and my past when I realized I needed help. I could not do it alone any longer. Are you ready to stop just being a survivor and become a warrior in your own life? Are you ready to heal? Are you ready to choose you? Are you ready to peel off all the layers and gunk that has been piled on you and reveal the gem and masterpiece that God uniquely created you to be? Reach out your hand and ask for help! I hope to be that hand for you and many others in the future!

PART 3

Going All In

CHAPTER 12

Glory Time

In March of 2024, I sat in a conference room at the Opryland Hotel in Nashville, Tennessee, with about 200 entrepreneurs, speakers, and coaches for The Movement Maker Live 2024 event put together and executed by the UnleashU Now team. My sister Smryna had invited herself to be my plus one, without any idea of what she was signing up for. She believed she was going to have a weekend of sightseeing and Nashville shenanigans while I attended the conference. She made the decision to attend the opening ceremony with me and both of our lives were changed in that moment and in that decision. I arrived with zero expectations as did she, but what followed during that weekend was nothing short of divine accordance.

That first evening we were captivated by each speaker that took the stage and we took notes vigorously trying to soak in all that was being shared. The vulnerability, trust, and hunger for personal and professional growth was palpable within each individual in attendance. We spent the next two days in pure awe; something special was happening in that room. The UnleashU family that had created the event, and every speaker they invited to the stage, was unabashedly pouring into each of us and unknowingly meeting each of us exactly where we were. This is a gift, not a learned skill.

I found myself inspired, encouraged, excited and scared shitless! My brain was vigorously churning, evaluating my personal and professional life. My heart was racing with anticipation and angst! Then it happened. It was during an overcoming limiting beliefs exercise with one of the speakers, Tiffany Clevinger, that I intentionally stepped into and accepted God's appointment for me and my life in a fresh and new way. Tiffany asked us to write on an arrow our limited belief. I wrote "I can't do it all." Tiffany held one end, and I placed the other end in the small V notch in my neck. I took a deep breath and took one huge step directly into it snapping the arrow into several pieces! It was at that very moment that I shattered that limiting belief! I could do it all! But what did that even mean?

About two years earlier, I had decided to get my Life and Health Coaching Certification and upon completion I had eagerly started my coaching business. My first social media post about my new business brought several clients and I was elated! I began a Self Care and Mindfulness group coaching program and clients signed up. Then a few months into it, life happened. I made the very difficult decision to leave my then fiancé Stan. That relationship wasn't perfect, but it offered me safety, financial stability, love and a future, but I was isolated from my friends, family and community. I had a moment in my home office when I looked in the mirror and realized that here I was charging people money and teaching them authenticity, alignment with your highest self and self-love, yet I was not in alignment with who I was nor who I wanted to be. Four days later, I packed a U-Haul and made the drive home from the beautiful foothills of the Blue Ridge Mountains of Virginia to the support of my tribe in North Carolina.

Upon arriving in North Carolina, I settled in quickly and went back to work trying to build my business. But everything I did seemed to fizzle. I had several amazing opportunities cross my path during that time. I became a contributing author in the Amazon Best Selling anthology *Breaking the Silence: Voices of Survivors.* My story was also published in the Amazon Best Selling book *Resilient AF: Stories of Resilience* published by the Global Resilience Project. I shared my story on over a dozen podcasts, and I had a couple of speaking opportunities where I had the opportunity to make an almost decade long dream come true.

I had felt the calling some ten years prior that I was destined to use my voice and my healing journey to help others, and I was finally doing it. Back then, I saw myself on a stage, I saw myself signing books, and I saw myself deep in the trenches with others that had experienced similar trauma that needed my God-given light and my journey in order to see their own light and healing. The only problem was, I wasn't making money, and I was bleeding money to be part of these cool opportunities! Thankfully, I could fall back on my giftings as a seasoned therapeutic massage therapist with over 17 years of experience and a dedicated client following. But that became physically taxing very quickly. I also began helping out part time in a medical office to make ends meet. It didn't take long for exhaustion to settle in. I was working three jobs, yet I was still stressed about how I was going to pay my rent every month. I was running, literally and figuratively!

In December of 2023 the universe sent another twist. I met a man on Facebook and we fell in love. From the first time we met, we both noticed a kismet connection on a soul level. Neither of us had experienced this before. Our relationship started out like a Hallmark movie. It felt like everything I had prayed for and the bonus was that he had a daughter!

Loren was a family man, a great communicator, a hard worker, a man of his word, loyal and trustworthy and he wanted to add to his family. Score! I was all in! We began spending every moment together that we weren't working. We talked, laughed, played music, played tennis, sang, played guitar and piano, and sat around philosophizing, and planning our future. We became intoxicatingly entangled! I began looking for other jobs so that I could stop running in three different directions all the time. I began trying to convince myself that I could live this life, but there were many red flags.

First, we didn't share the same passion and vigor for a personal relationship with God. He believed in God, but he felt abandoned by God.

Secondly, he didn't believe in the institution of marriage; he felt it was just a piece of paper and for him a true commitment to share a bank account and build a life together was more than that piece of paper. I wanted marriage, an engagement, a wedding, all of it. I had shared my desire for marriage and he had promised it would happen eventually. He said once that when we got married it would just be spontaneous and we would go down to the courthouse and just do it. He also stated he wasn't spending money on a ring and that I should be happy with whatever he gave me because it would come from love. I was conflicted, because on the one hand he was correct, I didn't need materialistic things, but for some reason that conversation felt yucky in my spirit, but I said nothing. I loved him and he was very good to me, and he made me feel like no other partner ever had in so many ways.

Thirdly, he saw everything as black and white. This was extremely hard for me because I felt like my whole life had been around color and shades of gray, there was no absolute other than God. Several times we had discussed this, but to no avail. He was indignant that everything

126

was either black or white. This statement seemed to come from a place of judgment and my spirit struggled with it. Everything could not be put in one of these two boxes and tied with a pretty bow.

Next, he would tell me that I "was his everything." This scared me, and I told him so. I would explain that I wasn't comfortable being his everything because that was a lot of pressure and I knew that I would disappoint him eventually. He insisted that is how he loved. I came to the relationship complete. I had family, friends, community and Loren did not have much of any of that to speak of, so I became his everything.

Lastly, he didn't like when I would travel and he became depressed and sad because he missed me. I shared with him from the beginning that I traveled for my job, and he was fine with that until we started talking about a family. He was firm that I couldn't travel if I had a baby. See, I could not do it all or have it all!

About five months into this intoxicating romance was when I attended the conference in Nashville. During the three-day conference, I realized that I had once again sacrificed who I was for someone else's dream. I wanted love, safety, security, stability and a family so badly that I was willing to give up my dreams of travel, speaking, and bringing my God-given message and light to those who needed it. I felt boxed in and afraid. How could I have him and all of our dreams and live my destiny at the same time?

The conference ended and Smyrna and I were packing up. She said she wanted to go speak to someone and I decided to mingle as well. Minutes later, I looked over and saw her talking to one of the speakers, Dr. Obom Bowen. I walked up and caught the tail end of their conversation. She then pointed to me and said, "This is my sister. She's really the one that needs to speak to you because she has a business and just needs help growing it." He turned to me and said, "Tell me about your business."

I began telling him of my woes and successes over the last 18 months. Then he stopped me and he said, "Have you heard of the book *Going All In?*" I looked at him sheepishly and said, "No, sorry, I never heard of you until this conference, so I haven't read any of your books." I assumed it was one of his many books that he had published. He smiled, shook his head and said, "It's not one of my books; it's yours!" I looked at him puzzled. What did he mean, my book? He continued, "It's also the name of your coaching program." "Ummm okay," I said with hesitance. "Also, you have to have it completed by the end of April, so it can be published and then I will have you on my stage for the Outcomes & Breakthroughs Mastermind in Florida June 5-9." I stared at him with tears welling up in my eyes. Was he for real? How? Really? What?" Mic drop! I stood there shaking with my hands covering my mouth. Unrestrained tears flowed from my eyes. He smiled and hugged me as I continued to cry onto his one-of-a-kind, specially made just for him button down shirt. All I could muster in that moment was "Thank you. Thank you for seeing me and believing in me. I needed this break, thank you!" We exchanged social media information and Smyrna and I said our heartfelt goodbyes to the UnleashU family and went on our way. With adrenaline pumping, and a small bounce in our step, we walked out of that conference knowing something magical had just happened. God had a divine appointment with me and had shared a message for my life through Dr. Obom and I had received it loud and clear. I could not have it all in the sense that I understood. I would have it all, but it meant I would have to let go and let God, because his plans are bigger, better and more spectacular than anything that we can plan or prepare ourselves for.

I returned home heavy hearted and absolutely elated at the same time. Dr. Obom had given me the swift kick in the ass that I needed and had lit the fuse. Now it was up to me. What would I do with this opportunity? Would I allow it to be the catalyst that propels me to the next level or would I fall back into what was comfortable? I began half-ass writing. Sadly, I fell right back into what had become my new norm with Loren and his daughter. But, something had changed in me during that three-day conference in Nashville. I was enormously afraid! I didn't know how to communicate these feelings to Loren, as they were all over the place. After all, he hadn't done anything outwardly wrong per say. But, I had caught a glimpse of my true self again, and had stepped out of the box of his dream, and back into my own reality. I had to choose me, my dreams, my purpose, and my future! I was euphoric at the new possibilities of bringing my testimony and message to the world and following my dreams that I had been working on for almost a decade. I began earnestly seeking God for clarity. Be careful when you pray for clarity, because God answers prayers but you don't get to choose how he does it or how painful it will be.

My clarity came one week after the conference ended. Loren and his daughter had a huge argument that triggered me in a way that I hadn't experienced for years, and I removed myself from the situation. I ended the relationship that night. In processing the evening's events, I quickly realized that this isolated incident was my emotional breaking point, and my way out. It would be a few days before I would realize that when I was in Nashville, I had stepped back into my authenticity and now I was being required to live it, and that is why I left. I am not proud of the way I left, as I felt the burden of the betrayal that Loren and his daughter felt. I had always been honest with him and did everything from a place of love, and gave all I was to the both of them, but I had placated my own dreams and desires and in the end that means I had been dishonest with them.

My healing journey continues with each life lesson, but so does my testimony. Furthermore, in releasing that relationship, I made space within myself to step fully into the process of writing this book and creating my trauma recovery coaching program. Without its release, I did not have the emotional, physical or spiritual bandwidth for executing this monumental task of writing a book! The days following our breakup, the creative energy started flowing and this book began to write itself. Everything inside me was ready to come out; it was divine timing and there was no stopping me, I was going all in. Within days of my breakup, my Mentor Dr. Loren Michaels Harris introduced me to two publishers, and I instantly connected with Lynda Sunshine West of Action Takers Publishing. She saw my dream and vision and we joined forces to create and make tangible something I had been carrying around and nurturing inside of me for well over a decade.

One morning while in Nashville preparing for another day of our Movement Makers 2024 conference, I looked at my sister while blow drying my hair. She appeared to be deep in thought. "What are you thinking about,?" I asked Smyrna. Without a moment of hesitation she said, "I was just wondering why you got to have all the trauma?" "Ummmm, what?," I said. She continued, "God loved you so much that he gave you all the different trauma so that when you healed you would be able to be a beacon of light for so many others in their trauma!" Wow, holy crap! She was right! That was a powerful moment!

But, can I be real with you? No, I mean real real, like raw real? Ok, here goes! Life is hard! Life hurts sometimes! It knocks you down, steals your breath, and leaves you wondering, really??? Why God!!! Ouch! That hurts!!!! Can I get a break!!! Again??? Another lesson? WHY??? Healing is hard too! There is zero instant gratification in healing; it's a marathon not a sprint. Then the moment comes and, Okay, God, I get it!!! My story, your glory! I'm ready. God did indeed love me so much, and now it was time for me to step into all he had created and prepared me for.

Glory: Going All In was born of this divinely exhilarating yet very painful experience of healing. Glory is my middle name. Although I was given the name Martha Glory by Cultman a few days after my birth, I have come to embrace and understand the power in my name. Unbeknownst to Cultman, in giving me my name he declared the Glory of God and his promises upon my life always! The acronym I have given Glory is God's Love Overflows Re-storying You. Your story is not over! That old story does not define you! Write your own! You can choose to change the narrative! This is the focus of my Trauma Recovery Coaching Program Going All In.

"Going All In" is a transformative faith-based trauma recovery program designed to guide individuals on a journey of healing and restoration. Rooted in the principles of faith and resilience, this program empowers you to fully commit to your recovery process, embracing every aspect of your journey with courage, hope, and determination. Through a combination of therapeutic self-reidentification techniques, spiritual guidance, and nurturing support, you are equipped with the resources and tools to confront your trauma, reidentify with self, rebuild your life, and step boldly into a future filled with purpose and wholeness.

Healing is a choice. Becoming a warrior is a choice! Are you waiting to really live and heal until things slow down or get easier or are you jumping in faith first? Not feet first, faith first! Enough! Stop making excuses!!! Each excuse is more wasted time keeping you from your purpose and fulfillment! You are one decision away from that moment! What will be your Go All In moment? Right now, do you have the courage to trust in the power of faith and believe and reclaim who God has created you to be with all your brokenness and resilience? If the answer is yes, then it's time for a breakthrough. I am here to help you! We are Going All In!

CHAPTER 13

Going All In

In the world of gambling, there's a game called Texas Hold 'em. This game has become very popular among both professional and amateur poker players. Each player has stacks of chips which the player can bet some or all of on a given hand. The best hand wins all the chips bet by all the players on that hand. One can also win all the chips if the player can "bluff" the other players into believing the "bluffer" has a winning hand. A player can bet any amount on a given hand which other players must match to stay in the hand. A player who believes he has the best hand or "bluffs" that he has the best hand may "go all in," meaning he bets all his chips that he has the best hand or that he can "bluff" the other players into dropping out.

In life "going all in" is also a gamble with potentially high risks and rewards. In life "bluffing" is a bad idea and being exposed may be much worse than losing a pile of chips. The courage and strength to "go all in" comes from our healing, education, experience, practice, training; but most of all, the strength comes from our collective experiences, the people in one's life who inspire, encourage and impact us in a profound way.

One such person inspired my father many years ago. This is how my dad retells the story. During our cult years, the group sometimes attended services at black churches in Pensacola, Florida. On one occasion, the group attended a worship service at a small Four Square Gospel church pastored by Rev. Hosea Bell. The church was a small old "clapboard" wooden structure in very poor repair. On the exterior, the paint was all peeling off. Inside was a little better but the spartan fixtures and hard wooden pews spoke to the poverty of the church and its parishioners.

It was a Sunday morning and the small number of worshipers were in their "Sunday best," bright and clean but a little threadbare. In the front of the church was an elevated stage with a single large "throne" chair covered in red velvet with gold painted woodwork. The chair was clearly a hand-me-down from a more prosperous time and place. After a brief sermon, Pastor Bell turned the proceeding over to a church woman to sing a solo hymn. My dad does not recall the woman's name, but "I can't forget her appearance. She was an enormous woman who filled the "throne chair" to full capacity and more. She was missing most of her front teeth and her face told the story of a tough life which was approaching its conclusion." He continues, "By any standard measure, this was a very unattractive human, the kind I would go out of my way to avoid. But... then something beautiful and amazing happened. She took the microphone and commenced to pour her heart out in a way that has made a lasting imprint on my soul for over 50 years. She simply sang the same refrain over and over with progressively more passion. "Lord Jesus is getting me ready for that great day." As she swayed back and forth, sweat began to pour out as the Holy Spirit of the Lord took over and transformed this "ugly" woman into a beautiful glowing "child of God."" Dad further recalls, "As the spirit flooded the room, I felt like I was floating off the wooden pew with a tingling sensation I had never known or felt before. I quickly realized what was so moving and inspirational about the soloist's singing. She believed what she was singing with her whole being." Dad was changed that day and has gone "all in" thanks to that woman (and many others).

When we encounter people who truly believe and live in their authenticity and God-given gifts and talents, the strength of their belief becomes part of us, because we are all part of the collective. Sometimes to truly see it and experience it we will be required to overcome initial biased impressions which blind us and keep us from feeling the beauty within.

The principles of the "Going All In" Coaching Program are simple, applicable and if done consistently will be helpful resources and tools in your healing toolbelt. Choosing to heal from trauma using the "Going All In" principles brings a multitude of benefits that extend far beyond mere recovery. By making the conscious decision to embark on your own transformative journey, you open yourself up to a world of possibilities.

Before we jump into the "Going All In" principles, I want to ask you a few questions and help you with some preliminary work to make sure you are motivated and prepared and will get the most out of the program. As you embark on this journey of self-discovery and healing, you will want to take the time to ask yourself and really be present with what comes up as you delve into the following questions. It's best if you write down your answers or type them so that you can refer back to them from time to time.

Warning, the following exercise requires vulnerability, and the ability to set your ego aside and just be present. Face what comes up with curiosity and understand that this is your life. There are no wrong answers! Focus on what resonates and feels worthy of further exploration.

First, it is essential to reconnect with your reason to live. This may sound weird, silly or woo woo, but so many of us go through life with zero intentionality and basically just let life pass us by. So first ask yourself these questions:

- Why do I get out of bed?
- Do I know my purpose?
- What are my gifts and talents?
- What sets my soul on fire?

As you take time to ask yourself these questions, I want you to remember, this spiritual experience in human form is a privilege. Just think about that for a minute. Are you treating your life like it's a privilege?

Gladys McGarey, MD, in her book *The Well-Lived Life*, succinctly shares this idea that you must have a reason to live! She writes, "Each of us is here for a reason, to learn and grow and to give our gifts. When we are able to do so, we're filled with the creative life energy that I call the "juice." The juice is our reason for living. It's our fulfillment, our joy. It's what happens when life is activated by love. It's the energy we get from the things that matter and mean something to us." So what is your juice?

Next, your healing is a choice that starts with surrender. The definition of surrender is to "yield or give up control or possession of something, typically as a result of a situation that renders resistance or opposition futile. In a broader sense, surrender can also refer to relinquishing oneself to a higher power, accepting circumstances beyond one's control, or submitting to a particular course of action or belief. Surrender often entails letting go of resistance, releasing attachment to outcomes, and embracing a sense of trust, humility, and acceptance. It can be both a conscious choice and a transformative process, allowing individuals to find peace, liberation, and inner strength amidst life's challenges."

The act of surrender must be a conscious choice. When it comes to your healing, surrendering to that which is greater than you is monumental, and the faster you realize that you cannot do it on your own the more quickly you will have the wisdom to embrace the journey of healing and all it entails. Question: What does surrender look like to you? Are you ready to ask for help?

After surrender, you must make the deliberate, intentional decision to choose to heal. Disclaimer, healing from your past, breaking generational cycles and reclaiming your identity, body, mind, and spirit is hard! It is not for the lazy or faint of heart. It is a process with many highs and lows. It is extremely painful at times. It requires you to be your own advocate and fight harder for yourself than you have fought for anything before. You have to feel to heal, which means during the process of releasing your traumas, and your past, you will be uncomfortable, you will want to run, you will want to numb, you will want to quit! It's a very lonely journey because no one can do the work except you! Question: Are you ready to heal? Are you ready to commit to the work required for your healing? Do you feel worthy of your healing?

If so, what's the feeling that you are connected to that makes you desire healing? In my experience, you have to be connected to a feeling so deeply that it roots itself in your consciousness and propels you forward every time you stumble. Without it, you will fall for anything and any positive momentum will come to a crashing halt. So if it's so hard and brutal, why choose to heal?

Because you are worth it! You are perfect and wonderfully made by God. You are destined for more than staying stuck in your pain and your past. You are not defined by those things or your trauma. You are not defined by what has been done to you, or the mistakes that you have made, or the hearts that you may have broken. In the book, *Many Lives Many Masters,* Brian L. Weiss, MD, explains with such precision this idea that we are perfectly and wonderfully made. He states, "It's as if a large diamond were to be found inside each person. Picture a diamond a foot long, the diamond has a thousand facets but the facets are covered with dirt and tar. It is the job of the soul to clean each facet until the surface is brilliant and can reflect a rainbow of colors. Now, some have cleaned many facets and gleam brightly, others have only managed to clean a few, they do not sparkle so. Yet underneath the dirt each person possesses within his or her breasts a brilliant diamond with a thousand gleaming facets. The diamond is perfect, not one flaw. The only differences among people are the number of facets cleaned. But each diamond is the same and each is perfect. When all the facets are cleaned and shining forth in a spectrum of lights the diamond returns to the pure energy that it was originally, the lights remain. It is as if the process that goes into making the diamond is reversed. All that pressure released. Pure energy exists in the rainbow of lights and the lights possess consciousness and knowledge, and all the diamonds are perfect." So, your trauma, your pain, your past, your fears, your excuses and everything else that is holding you back from taking the needed steps to heal, is the dirt and tar. So make the choice, you are a diamond!

Choosing and embracing inner healing facilitates a profound sense of empowerment and a new self-awareness of your capabilities. This allows you the courage and fortitude to stand up strong and proud and say, "Enough! I am ready to take back and reclaim control over my life and I am ready to rewrite my story! My narrative changes today! I am not my past; I am the future that I will create! As of this moment, I am stepping into who God says I am!"

As you delve deeper into the healing process, you will discover newfound resilience and strength, honing the tools necessary to navigate life's challenges with grace and humility. Moreover, by addressing and processing past traumas and allowing for inner healing, you pave the way for emotional liberation! This liberation frees you from the shackles of the pain from your past and fosters a greater sense of peace and well-being. Ultimately, the "Going All In" Trauma Recovery Coaching Program not only facilitates inner healing but it also cultivates personal growth and development, self-awareness, self-love and courage enabling you to step into your fullest God-given potential in order to live a life of love, passion, purpose, authenticity, and joy.

Choosing all of these things previously mentioned, purpose, juice, surrender, inner healing, etc. is most importantly choosing you! The most important investment you will ever make is in yourself. The relationship with yourself must be the most precious and well-maintained relationship in your life. If you love your spouse, children, friends, pets, community with all your heart, then you must love yourself even more in order to give them from your overflow.

As a recovering caretaker and nurturer of others, I found joy and purpose in taking care of and nurturing others but over time I became exhausted, worn out and irritable! Why? Because I wasn't giving myself the same love and attention I was giving to others so I was empty, dry and wrung out! This got my attention. But it took more time than I would like to admit before I allowed this idea to sink in and I really made a change. I felt selfish, I felt in turmoil and in conflict with who I innately was born to be. I was born with a servant's heart. I love everyone and love to serve! There is nothing that brings me more joy than nurturing, supporting and loving on those that God has put in my pathway. But I cannot take care of others if I don't take care of myself first! I cannot be of service to others if I do not first be of service to myself. I cannot wholly love others if I do not first wholly love myself. It's just that simple.

Changing that mindset and creating healthy habits to support this new mindset was challenging at first, but the more consistently I did it, the easier it became. But, just to be transparent and in all honesty, I still catch myself from time to time falling back into my old caretaker ways and inevitably I begin to suffer the sacrifice. When that happens, I quickly recalibrate and redirect my energy inward in order to fill me back up so I can give from my overflow. I want you to keep this idea in mind as we dive into the "Going All In" principles.

Let's jump right into the Principles The acronym for "Going All In" is as follows:

G: God

O: Overcoming Obstacles

I: Inner Healing

N: Nurturing Accountability and Support

G: Grace filled forgiveness

A: Anchored

L: Love

L: Living on Purpose

I: Intentional Growth

N: New Beginnings

CHAPTER 14

The Principles

G - God

The first principle of the "Going All In" Trauma Recovery Coaching Program is G - God. Choosing God on your trauma recovery journey means embracing that which is greater than you and finding strength and safety in knowing that all things are working together for your highest good. This is faith! Faith is believing in what you know to be true unconditionally. Without being able to see it, but knowing with every cell of your being that it is there! Faith is a feeling, a knowing and a realization that you are never really alone. Without faith, healing is harder, and even more lonely.

On this journey there will be times that literally all you have is God. Feeling and cultivating a personal relationship will allow you to feel his love, guidance, and promises for your life. It means finding solace and strength in his presence throughout the healing process. As I stated above, healing is lonely, but you are never truly alone because God is always with you and for you. He knew you before the beginning of time; he knew you in your mother's womb! He knows and loves you like only God can. Healing starts with God because all healing comes from God. We can do the work, but without God it will not last.

Brian Weiss, MD in *Messages from the Masters* drives home this idea: "It may seem strange to hear a psychiatrist talking about God and love. Yet I must, because the foundations of spiritual psychotherapy require the recognition of our Divinity, the real nature of our souls, and the true purpose of existence here in physical form. Only in this way can we see the bigger picture. Without love and without God, there is nothing. God does not require our respect. He persists in personifying God, despite our knowledge that God is far beyond what we can even begin to conceptualize. God is everything, a loving energy possessing incomprehensible wisdom, power, and unknowable qualities. We are all composed of God, for God is in each of us and the substance of our being. God is peace; God is love. We have forgotten that since we are created in the divine image, God is within our hearts, and that we are also creatures of peace, beings of love and divinity."

Choosing God means choosing yourself! Denying God means denying yourself, because we are all created in the image of God. Woah! That's deep! Sit with that for a moment.

Choosing God in your healing journey offers a profound pathway to lasting restoration of our mind, body and spirit. By embracing God's presence and guidance, you invite divine wisdom and comfort into your life and journey. Choosing God means placing trust in something that is bigger than you. It's understanding and accepting His infinite love and sovereignty, then finding solace in His promises of healing, peace and redemption. Through practices such as prayer, meditation, reading faith-filled texts and other spiritual focused practices, you will deepen and strengthen your personal relationship with God. In flexing this relationship, you discover a source of strength and resilience that transcends human limitations. It is also helpful to join or to interact with a supportive faith-based community where individuals can lift you up, share your burdens, and experience the transformative power of collective faith. Romans 12:15 says, "Rejoice with those who rejoice, weep with those who weep." We are not meant to do life alone; we are meant for community.

Ultimately, choosing God is an affirmation of hope, faith, and the belief that with Him, all things are possible, and healing is not just a destination but a sacred journey toward wholeness and purpose. God's plans for your life are always bigger, better and more profound than anything you can dream up on your own, but it requires you to Go All In!

O - Overcoming Obstacles

The next principle is overcoming obstacles. Through the lens of faith, you will learn to navigate challenges with an unwavering trust in a higher power who always has your best and highest interest at heart. Overcoming obstacles requires you to stretch and build your ability to be resilient and stand in your faith when you are feeling weak. With resilience as your guiding light, you will confront obstacles head-on, knowing that setbacks are opportunities for growth and learning. When you are feeling weak, leaning into your faith will cultivate a deep sense of inner resilience, allowing you to persevere through adversity with courage and determination. Just as with the first principle, through prayer, meditation, and connection to a supportive faith-based community, you will discover the power of resilience as you navigate the complexities of healing and recovery. "Going All In" and overcoming obstacles with faith and resilience isn't just about conquering challenges—it's about embracing the journey with trust, hope, and a steadfast belief in the transformative power of the divine purpose within YOU. It's an amazing and powerful feeling when you understand in the depths of your soul that God's got your back and that you are destined for greatness! You, as a creation of God, are more powerful than you can even fathom. You are resilient and have the ability to navigate and overcome all that life throws at you, but you have to tap into your energy source! It all starts by going "In."

I - Inner Healing

Inner healing is the next principle. This principle is the 2nd most important principle after God and love in the Going All In program. Going inward is so much more important than healing the outside, our physical body. You can work out, change your hair, release weight, get liposuction or Botox, or do anything else to improve your outward appearance, but if you don't heal the inner you, you will never embody or embrace the outer you. That's why fad diets don't work long term. Most people can take off the weight but then they put it right back on. Keeping it off takes internal work. Lifestyle changes, mindset shifts, habit change, creating new neural pathways in place of old patterns, self-love, self-awareness and just an overall desire to do what it takes to become a healthier, happier you for the rest of your life.

Embracing inner healing is a sacred and transformative process guided by faith and spiritual principles. It is the hardest, yet the most fulfilling healing work that you will do. Understanding and connecting to your inner healing allows you to tap into the unique individual that God created you to be. It's in this process that we are required to tear off and peel away all the labels, limitations, expectations, and all the other things that no longer serve you. Then having the courage to take one giant step into your God-given gifts, purpose and divine healing.

The journey inward allows you to explore, accept and forgive your past with courage and vulnerability. Through prayer, meditation, journaling and reflection, you will create a sacred space for healing to unfold in the deepest, darkest valleys and crevices of your soul. You will also learn to release pent-up emotions, forgive yourself and others, and let go of fear, shame, guilt and any other burdens weighing heavily on your mind, body and spirit. With support, you will discover the healing power of divine grace for yourself and others.

Grace will allow you to experience a profound sense of freedom from that which has held you back and will elevate to a sense of newness and renewal. Choosing inner healing means surrendering to the transformative work of God's love, and allowing that to become self love. In doing this you will re-identify with Self in a deep and life giving way. Self love is what mends the broken pieces of our souls and restores wholeness from within. Our self-love is the measurement by which we will tolerate how others treat us. If we mistrust and are disloyal to ourselves and beat ourselves up about our weight, mistakes, beliefs, and our past etc. we will allow others to abuse us in the same way. Learning self-love and treating yourself in a worthy and positive way will teach others to treat you in the same way. We can not learn these things without looking inward first.

N - Nurturing Accountability and Support

Nurturing accountability and support is an integral part of all healing journeys. We need accountability and support on our healing journeys to encourage us, keep us focused, remind us of our worth when we can't see it, and to keep us accountable to ourselves. This is one of my favorite roles as a Coach. I get to walk alongside you, giving you resources and teaching you tools, but most importantly I have the privilege of keeping you accountable to yourself! I resonate on such a deep level with my clients and have the innate ability to hold space for them because I have been there! I have shared experiences and I have done and am continuing to do the work! I love supporting and encouraging my clients when they want to quit because I know exactly how they feel! I tried to quit a thousand times! We are not meant to do life alone; we need support.

Humans are meant for community; we are meant for the collective. Incorporating nurturing accountability and support on your healing journey allows you to have a safe space to be open, vulnerable and transparent while acknowledging, feeling and working through your struggles, past and traumas.

Another benefit of nurturing accountability and support is the ability to seek guidance when needed. This allows you to actively participate in your own recovery process, but having the built-in framework and protection from your saboteurs. Additionally, creating a nurturing environment of support is crucial for facilitating healing. In short, your accountability and support person or people provide compassionate encouragement, empathetic listening, and practical assistance to you while navigating the challenges of your healing and your life. This will empower you to confront your challenges with resilience and faith, knowing that you are not alone in this journey towards healing. As humans, we are all connected, and are all parts of a bigger whole. Understanding that you can share and lean on and gain introspection, encouragement and tools from those you surround yourself with is Gold!

We are all part of the collective! Gladys McGarey, MD in *The Well Lived Life* explains it this way, "By collective purpose, I don't mean that we all have the same purpose. Rather, I mean that when we're juiced, we contribute to the greater sense of purpose that ripples out from those with whom we interact to our greater community. Our individual souls are like pieces of a jigsaw puzzle. Our purpose locks us together, creating something greater and more beautiful than any of us could achieve alone." We are stronger together as the collective than we can ever be on our own.

I have been so blessed on my journey to have many amazing people that have come alongside me and loved and supported me when I couldn't see my path clearly. God has strategically placed people in my life for specific purposes. Some have been in my life for a long time, and others for a very short time, but I have still felt the positive impact of not having to do life alone. There is something powerful about surrounding yourself with people that will pray with you and for you, that love you wholly and completely without judgment and support your hopes and dreams as if they were their own. I owe a huge thank you to my nurturing support and accountability people: my parents/ siblings/and extended family (you know who you are, as there are too many to name, this includes my brothers and sister in-laws), StacyRae J., Shanna K., Bridget D., Ally N., Meghan G., Phyllis & Keith Y., Nana & Kendrick V., Jamie T., Noelle R., Bonnie M., Naomi B., Rashmi & Nikin S., and Priya & Devan P. Each of you have touched my life in a personal and meaningful way, and I am eternally grateful.

G - Grace-Filled Forgiveness

The principle of "Grace-Filled Forgiveness" is foundational and fundamental to the healing process of self. This was one of the most difficult principles for me to grasp! Pain is heavy, scars are ugly, regrets are torturous, and all are wasted energy. Author Matthew Ichihashi Potts in *Forgiveness: An Alternative Account* shares, "Forgiveness reckons unflinchingly with a past that cannot be undone. The futility of retribution's urge to turn time backwards is precisely what forgiveness understands and works against." Embracing the concept of forgiveness as an essential component of your healing journey towards wholeness is essential. This involves extending grace and forgiveness to yourself first, which generally is difficult because we feel undeserving. Next is extending it to others. Terah Shelton Harris, in her book *One Summer in Savannah* writes, "Forgiveness can be a powerful tool. It can loosen the knots we often tie ourselves. It can heal trauma, visible and invisible. But withholding forgiveness can also cause more harm than good. It can tighten its grip on you, binding you to the person who hurt you."

The benefit of extending grace-filled forgiveness is releasing resentment, pain, anger, and bitterness that may be holding you or them back and allowing peace, love and joy to take its place. Through faith, you will learn to tap into the transformative power of forgiveness, recognizing that it is not about excusing or condoning past actions but rather about freeing yourself from the burden of pain and resentment that is keeping you shackled to the past or that event. By embracing grace-filled forgiveness, you will experience profound freedom and inner peace, allowing you to move forward on your path toward healing with renewed hope and resilience. Forgiveness is so powerful, and it's free to all! But it is a muscle that must be built, flexed and used in order to keep it sharpened. Martin Luther King, Jr. said, "Forgiveness is not an occasional act; it is a permanent attitude."

A - Anchored

The principle of "Anchored" emphasizes the importance of finding stability, security, peace and your reason for desiring and being on your healing journey. In the context of the "Going All In" Trauma Recovery Coaching Program, an "anchor" refers to a psychological technique or strategy used to evoke a specific state of mind or emotion. It's a tool that helps you access desired feelings or resources, such as calmness, confidence, or resilience, by associating them with a particular sensory cue or mental image. Anchors can be created through repeated practice and association, linking an external stimulus (such as a word, gesture, or object) with an internal state or experience. When triggered, anchors can help you shift your mindset, manage difficult emotions, and/or access inner strengths during challenging situations.

In order to heal, you must anchor yourself for and to a purpose which is bigger than yourself, or you will quit as soon as it gets hard. Being anchored and rooted firmly in your faith, purpose, goals and positive beliefs is essential. When you are anchored to something and in something, it serves as a firm foundation that grounds you especially during times of difficulty or uncertainty. For example, being anchored to faith can provide comfort, guidance, and hope during times of adversity, setbacks or painful life happenings fostering a deeper sense of connection and purpose. Ultimately, being anchored to something positive means finding strength and solace in that aspect of your life, allowing it to support and uplift you as you journey towards healing and wholeness. Another example is having an anchor that is something tangible or that you desire, like a picture, screensaver, book, statue, piece of jewelry, knick knack or whatever you can quickly connect with to anchor yourself when life throws you a curveball.

I love sunflowers and my favorite color is yellow. I have sunflowers everywhere in my home, car and office. Sunflowers are an anchor for me because every time I see them when I am in need of an anchor, I remember the way they make me feel when I look at them. I feel joy, happiness, peace, safety, strength and love. Sunflowers symbolize vitality and growth, and they are bright and cheery. Sunflowers anchor me to my healing journey. I love the following quotes and have them posted in several places as a constant anchor. "A sunflower does not compete with other flowers; it just blooms." And another, "Like a sunflower, always follow the light within you and bloom boldly." Lastly, "Sunflowers end up facing the sun, but they go through a lot of dirt to find their way there."

L - Love

Our next principle is Love. You cannot heal without love. God and love are synonymous and are the most important principles on our healing journey. Within this principle, we discuss love of self and love for and from others. Love must start with and from self. We can't authentically and purely love someone else if we don't first love ourselves. When we experience love—whether it's from God, friends, or family—it has the power to heal wounds, mend brokenness, and restore a sense of wholeness to our lives that no other principle can do, but we must have the courage to give that love to ourselves first. Do you love yourself? Do you know what it means to truly and authentically love and have a personal relationship with yourself?

The love of self is the most important love we will ever experience. Our capabilities and ability to love God and others will always be second to how much we are willing to love ourselves and find ourselves worthy of that love. In the book *The Mastery of Love*, by Don Miguel Ruiz he explains the importance of self love. "You are what you believe you are. There is nothing to do except to be just what you are. You have the right to feel beautiful and enjoy it. You can honor your body and accept it as it is. You don't need anyone to love you. Love comes from the inside. It lives inside us and is always there, but with that wall of fog, we don't feel it. You can only perceive the beauty that lives outside you when you feel the beauty that lives inside you. You have a belief about what is beautiful and what is ugly, and if you don't like yourself, you can change your belief and your life will change. It. Sounds simple, but it isn't. Whoever controls the belief, controls the dream. When the dreamer finally controls the dream, the dream can become a masterpiece of art. Just imagine how you will feel the day you adore your own body. When you accept yourself completely, you will feel so good about your own body, and you are going to be so happy. Then when you relate with someone else, your limit of self-abuse is almost zero. This is self-love. This is not personal importance because you treat others with the same love, the same honor, the same respect, and the same gratitude you use with yourself."

Love provides a nurturing environment in which healing can take place, offering acceptance, empathy, and understanding without judgment. It creates a sense of belonging and connection, reminding us that we are not alone in our pain and struggles. Love also fosters resilience, empowering us to face our challenges with courage and determination, knowing that we are supported and valued. Moreover, love teaches us to extend compassion and forgiveness to ourselves, allowing us to release self-blame and embrace our innate and divine worthiness. Ultimately, love is a guiding force on our healing journey, illuminating the path towards greater self-discovery, growth, and physical, emotional and spiritual well-being.

In *The Well-Lived Life*, Gladys McGarey, MD says this about love: "I hope you've had the chance to know how love can sweep in and change everything, overpowering anything in its presence. It's not hokey. It's not overstated. Love truly is the greatest medicine the world has ever known. It takes life from a passive State (being alive) to an active State (truly living). That's why love is the most powerful medicine. Our life force is activated by love." Love is medicine; it heals, restores and really has the ability to change everything.

The process of going from self awareness to liking myself to loving myself has been a grueling one. It was just so much easier to focus on loving others! What I realized in this process of relearning how to love myself, was that loving others was a Band-Aid for my inability to look at myself and accept myself just as I was. It kept me from being able to find the compassion to embrace that divine being for who she was and is and love her enough to find her worthy of self love. That was a HARD realization!!! But as I did the work and uncovered what it was that I didn't like about myself, I realized that all the things I didn't like were a response to something or someone else had done to me leaking their poison into my fresh water basin of self love. I was tainted by the opinions, words, beliefs and expectations of others. I had to release all of those things as they were not of me! It was time to siphon that water, and clean it out for good. I began to embrace myself, physically, emotionally, spiritually and verbally. If I found something I didn't like about myself, that was indeed mine then I made the intentional choice to change it or to let it go. The ripple effect of this choice to love myself wholly and completely mind, body and spirit is ongoing. There is never an arrival point but it does make the journey a whole lot more joy filled and worthwhile. It also allows me to love others and accept them just as they are in a deeper and more meaningful way.

My car license plate reads ILUVALL. I do try to live my life from a place of love for everyone and everything. But, I am not perpetuating the myth that just because you love all, doesn't mean that you have to tolerate bad behavior, or agree with something that doesn't resonate with you or spend time with someone that your energy is just not aligned with. NO! Because first you love yourself enough NOT to spend your energy on things that do not serve you or help you to grow. But you can still Love All! Loving all means you are able to see others and accept them as they are without assumptions or judgment, but also understanding your need to protect your peace. You love yourself enough to always put your peace first.

L - Living on Purpose

Our next principle is Living on Purpose. Living on Purpose is not merely existing; it is accepting and knowing with every fiber of your being what you were created for, what your gifts are and why only you are divinely chosen to deliver that purpose. As I shared earlier in this chapter, Gladys McGarey calls it the "juice." It's your life force, your motivation, your reason for getting out of bed. The act of Living on Purpose is a powerful aspect of one's healing journey, providing direction, meaning, and fulfillment as you navigate through life's ups and downs.

Living on Purpose is being in alignment with our highest self. When we live in alignment with our purpose, we are able to channel our energy and focus towards meaningful pursuits that resonate with our core values, dreams and aspirations. This sense of purpose serves as a guiding light, helping us to find clarity amidst the challenges we face and motivating us to persevere in spite of obstacles. Moreover, Living on Purpose allows us to transcend our pain and trauma by focusing on something greater than ourselves, whether it's contributing to the well-being of others, pursuing creative endeavors, or advocating for causes that are important to us.

By embracing our purpose, we tap into a source of inner strength and resilience that empowers us to overcome adversity and thrive in the face of hardship. Ultimately, Living on Purpose becomes a source of healing and transformation, enabling us to reclaim our power, find fulfillment, and create a life that is rich with meaning and significance. I remember sitting in my Life Coach's office about seven years ago and saying to him "Why, am I here? What is my purpose? There has to be more than this! I feel empty, unmotivated and frankly bored!" I had been on my healing journey for several years and outwardly I was doing much better. Physically I was pretty healthy, but inside I was searching! I spent the next couple of months with him discovering my purpose, passions, aspirations and setting goals. I found my "juice!" This life activating force served as a motivator and I had work to do before I could begin living in it and on purpose. I had to continue to uncover the diamond prongs and pour love and time into reclaiming "Self" so I could stand in my purpose and begin living my "juice."

I read a quote by Ethan Hawk that says, "Often we imagine that we will work hard...arrive at some distant goal, and then we will be happy. This is a delusion. Happiness is a result of a life lived with purpose. Happiness is not an objective. It is the movement of life itself, a process, and an activity." If you want to be happy, discover your purpose and Live on Purpose!

I - Intentional Growth

Intentional Growth is our second to last principle. Healing does not happen just because we want it to. It does not happen by proxy because someone else wants it for us. Healing is an intentional act which creates a ripple effect of growth in all aspects of our lives. Intentional growth is a vital component of one's healing journey. It empowers you to be an active participant in your own healing and transformation story.

When we commit to intentional growth, we make a conscious decision to cultivate positive change in our lives, regardless if they are comfortable or not. Often we must get comfortable with being uncomfortable so we can step into the new and updated version of ourselves. The positive change comes from embracing and loving yourself so much that you are willing to shift your limiting beliefs, let go of bad habits, and understand that when done consistently you can transform your life. This involves setting clear intentions, defining specific goals, and taking deliberate actions to expand our understanding, skills, and resilience.

Through intentional growth, we embrace opportunities for self-reflection and self-discovery, uncovering hidden strengths and potential within ourselves. We actively seek out experiences that challenge us to step outside of our comfort zones, confront our fears, and learn from our mistakes. As we continue to grow and evolve, we gain a deeper sense of self-awareness and empowerment, allowing us to navigate the complexities of healing with greater clarity, confidence, and resilience.

Ultimately, intentional growth becomes a catalyst enabling us to transform our pain into purpose and emerge from adversity stronger, wiser, and more resilient than we ever thought possible. A quote by Jim Rohn that really encapsulates this idea is, "You cannot change your destination overnight, but you can change your direction overnight. If you want to reach your goals and fulfill your potential, become intentional about your personal growth. It will change your life." This is precisely what happened to me in my life coach's office so many years ago. I uncovered my purpose, but could not dive into it overnight. I had to be patient and do the work, make the changes, get really uncomfortable and press on and that would eventually change my life.

N - New Beginnings

Our final principle is New Beginnings. Lamentations 3:22-23 says, "The steadfast love of the Lord never ceases, his mercies never come to an end; they are new every morning; great is your faithfulness." (New Revised Standard Version Bible, copyright © 1989 National Council of the Churches of Christ in the United States of America.) Every single breath we breathe is a chance for a new beginning. Embracing that concept and understanding that this moment is the only one that we have is essential for our overall healing. Don't put it off, as we are not promised tomorrow.

New beginnings are a fundamental aspect of one's healing journey because it symbolizes a fresh start and a hopeful outlook on the future. When you embark on a path of healing, you will often be confronted by past pain, traumas and challenges. Choosing a new beginning signifies seeking to release old wounds and patterns that no longer serve you, and stepping into the freshness and beauty of your chosen future. In embracing new beginnings, you courageously step into the unknown, leaving behind the pain and limitations of the past which allows you the space to embrace growth, renewal, healing and transformation.

Each new beginning offers an opportunity to redefine yourself, to rediscover passions and dreams that may have been dormant or overshadowed by challenges, pain or adversity. They also inspire you to set intentions, establish goals, and cultivate a vision for a life filled with purpose, joy, and fulfillment that you want and desire with everything that you are. As you learn to embrace new beginnings on your healing journey, you will be awakened to the endless possibilities that lie ahead and become empowered to create a future that is in alignment with our highest and most authentic self. Remember, all we have is this moment.

Each moment serves as an opportunity or challenge at a new beginning. All it takes is action. Meister Eckhart says, "And suddenly you just know it's time to start something new and trust the magic of beginning."

In conclusion, the principles of my "Going All In" Trauma Recovery Coaching Program embody a comprehensive and holistic approach to faith-based trauma healing, encapsulating nine fundamental principles that will guide you on a journey toward healing and transformation. The principles are presented in a particular order for the sake of the "Going All In" acronym, but it is not necessary to work through or practice them in this specific order. All of the principles are important, but there are a few that should be focused on first that will lend themselves to the next. Embrace the principles, trust yourself and the process and you will be on your way to a healthier, happier, more love-filled human experience.

The program begins with "God," emphasizing the importance of embracing faith and finding strength and solace in a higher power.

"Overcoming Obstacles" emphasizes resilience and unwavering trust in a divine purpose, empowering you to confront challenges head-on.

"Inner Healing" encourages deep introspection and self-awareness, facilitating the release of past wounds and limitations.

"Nurturing Accountability and Support" highlights the significance of community and guidance in fostering healing and growth.

"Grace-Filled Forgiveness" emphasizes the transformative power of extending grace and letting go of resentment and pain.

"Anchored" stresses the importance of finding stability and purpose.

"Love" underscores the healing potential of love for oneself and others.

"Living on Purpose" encourages you to embrace your unique gifts and passions, finding fulfillment and meaning in your journey.

"Intentional Growth" promotes deliberate self-improvement and resilience-building practices, leading to transformative personal growth.

"New Beginnings" symbolizes hope and renewal, encouraging you to embrace each moment as an opportunity for healing and transformation.

Combined, these principles provide a comprehensive framework for you to embark on a healing journey toward wholeness, guided by faith, love, resilience, and purpose.

About the Author

My name is Martha Glory Stecker Kartaoui. I was born and raised in a religious cult and I escaped when I was almost 26 years old. My transition into the real world was tricky and difficult. But as I creep up to my 20th anniversary of freeing myself from the clutches of Cultman, I look around with pride, joy and love. I have come a very long way. My healing journey has been arduous, uncomfortable and debilitating at times, but it was all worth it!

I am very proud of the woman that I have grown into and discovered that I am! I take time often to take a deep breath and allow myself to just feel the magnitude of the things that I have healed and overcome.

I am so happy to announce that most of my family is out of the cult and rebuilding their lives as well. The majority of my family resides in North Carolina near me, with a few sprinkles on the west coast and in Virginia. As a collective, we have worked hard and created a stronger familial bond than we ever had growing up because we all have a shared story and know what each family member has been through and we take nothing for granted. We still have one sister that remains in the cult, indoctrinated, brainwashed and controlled. It is always our sincere prayer that she rejoins our family at some point, but it will have to be her choice because we cannot save anybody from their journey. We continue to pray expectantly!

Papa has passed on now, but the gift he gave me lives on with me always. I know that he would be proud of me, and he would be my biggest cheerleader in this season of my life. I have also had the pleasure of getting to know my biological grandparents, aunts, uncles and cousins on both of my parents' sides. I have been embraced by most of them, and I am forever grateful to know the love and support of my extended family.

All of my grandparents have passed on now, but I am forever thankful for the time that we did have making memories and getting to know one another. A piece of me has healed having the opportunity to know and be loved by my extended family. Our lineage is important, and until I left the cult, that puzzle piece was missing. Growing up without my relatives was lonely and hard.

Innately we want to know where we come from, and my relatives equally wanted to know us. I am thankful for every opportunity that I get to spend time with them as it continues to heal what the cult tried to keep away from me. Auntie Barbara, Auntie Jill, Auntie Christi and Uncle Kurt, thank you for going out of your way to love, support and embrace me! It's been truly a gift to have you guys celebrating me and cheering me on.

I wear many hats. I am first and foremost a child of God, a daughter, sister, friend, Author, Coach, Speaker, Mentor, and Massage Therapist, but my favorite title is " auntie" and I am blessed with 11 nieces and nephews. Becoming an "Auntie" is the reason I found the courage, strength and will power to make my escape nearly 20 years ago. I am reminded of this blessing in each of my interactions with my beautiful nieces and nephews.

A couple of months ago, I celebrated my 45th birthday. Smyrna and StacyRae threw me a birthday party. Smyrna organized and gave me truly the most profound and amazing gift. I share it here for two reasons. First, this gift made me take a moment and really reflect on my healing journey. I am so proud of the work and healing that I have done and continue to do. I was determined, strong, courageous and resilient when the journey became difficult. I have found meaning and purpose in my suffering, and am dedicated to using those experiences to lift up others! Secondly, I share here because it touched my heart and soul in such a deep and meaningful way, and I am okay if you steal the idea and spread the love! So, what was the gift?

I love oatmeal. Smyrna took three boxes of oatmeal with 20 individual servings in each box and had my friends and family share their memories and thoughts about me. Then she carefully taped one message to each individual package, some packages ended up with two messages. Her request was that each day that I ate oatmeal, I would open the message on the pack. I followed her directions for about six days and then I had a really rough day, and I grabbed one of the boxes and sat at my kitchen table and read every single message. I laughed, I cried, and I even gasped a couple of times as I read each word printed on those slips of paper. In that moment, those words were a lifeline for me: words have power.

In short, we need our people, our tribe and our community! I am so grateful for mine. Last night I sat on my couch and opened the last box of oatmeal and read each heartfelt message written by my friends and family from near and far. I felt like my heart would explode from gratitude! Again, I laughed, and cried, but mostly I just let the words sink into my soul and wash over me like a wave of love ebbing and flowing with each message. These messages will be a keepsake, a prize possession and a reminder that I am loved, supported and ready to serve. What follows is some of those messages.

*Martha, It has been my honor to fulfill this crazy idea of mine and fill your 45th year of life with oatmeal that carries memories, love, life and laughter through messages from your family and friends! I love you sister!

*45 years ago, the Lord brought Martha into this world at my first home birth. My labor was long but not hard seeing her right away as a bundle with dark hair was a sight that I will never forget. The Lord continues to be with her and has prospered and allowed her to become an author, massage therapist, inspirational speaker and a life/health coach. She continues to amaze me and all that she touches. She has a heart of gold and is the most empathetic person that I know. She's on a path for great things and I am blessed to be her Mom.

*Martha is so positive to be around! She's nothing short of good vibes, always elevating the room she is in and the people she is with. She's a lot like a sweet and sour skittle to me, having a sweet and caring side, but boy can she have a little kick of sass with it, too!

*I love you Martha so much. You are so full of light and love and have always shown me undying love and support.

*To the most special person in the world... God put us together. Our friendship is something from biblical times and only something that we understand. God told me this: You are more than a friend, more than a sister, more than anything I can know or express. I love you!

*You are my absolute favorite. Your smile opens gateways. Your eyes see through to each soul. Your being holds space for so many. Keep showing up. I love you!

*Martha, Martha, Martha!! Your sunshine, your laughter, your sneeze! I love every bit of it with all my heart. I am so proud of you and beyond. I'm honored to have ever been graced to call you friend, boss, and lobster roll confidant. I appreciate how you've been the beacon, for not only my life, but now an inspirational speaker for millions of lives. Thank you to Infinity for being you. You are the best!

*You always bring a positive presence and perspective! You have a generous and genuine heart and a real sense for what people need in a particular moment. You give without the motivation or expectation of getting something in return.

*Why am I special? You may ask yourself. Perhaps because you know how to light up a room with just your presence. Could be because you love so big. It's undeniable to anyone around. You are the ultimate ray of sunshine. Maybe the way you present yourself, the way you move through life creating and protecting your own peace but also being exceptional at protecting any and everyone around you. Your license plate says it the most accurately. You love all and you do it incredibly well. Ultimately, what makes you the most genuine and amazing Auntie I could ever ask for, is just you being you. I love you forever, you are my reason and my tangible Sunshine.

*Martha, you are truly a gift from God to our family and all that know and have known you. Your energy brightens up every room you walk into. I still giggle every time I go to the Highlanders brewery thinking about the time you drank out of the creek with your life straw, then sat down on a rock and meditated! You're a bright light in this world!

*When I think of Martha, I just see this amazing light inside of her blossoming, and how she shows up for life no matter what, with deep integrity and intention. She's an inspiration for how to live. Incredibly impressed you chose to serve in China for your 40th birthday! Incredibly grateful we get to celebrate you on your 45th birthday!

*You are the freest of spirits, so much so that "no" and "can't" aren't exactly prevalent in your vocabulary. A memory that encapsulates that is the night we climbed to the top of the plowed snow mountain in the middle of the Food Lion parking lot, like no one was watching or would care that two grown women had decided to spur of the moment run up slick, snow and ice as tall as the building itself.

*Our shared love to travel, making memories, stressing each other out, making each other laugh, supporting and encouraging each other, unabashedly trying new things together are just a few reasons I feel immensely blessed to have you as my sister.

*Martha can make some good crack chicken. Martha can always help me through my problems and find solutions. Martha's like the sister I never had. Martha always thinks of others and has a way of explaining opposing views and helping me form tipsy speech into actual feelings.

I saved the best for last.

*Four score and five years ago in the Hamlet of Mankato, Minnesota, a determined child was delivered by a midwife. We met her on the occasion of her birth to determine if a child so conceived and so delivered could become a famous author, inspirational speaker, and evangelist. All the people said Amen. With apologies to Abe Lincoln. -Dad

I would like to end this book with a prayer from the book *The Mastery of Love* by Don Miguel Ruiz. I have read this prayer many times, and have prayed it even more times. I hope it blesses you the way that it blessed me.

"Today, Creator of the Universe-God, we asked that you help us to accept ourselves just the way we are, without judgment. Help us to accept our mind the way it is, with all our emotions, our hopes and dreams, our personality, our unique way of being. Help us to accept our body just the way it is, with all its beauty and perfection. Let the love we have for ourselves be so strong that we never again reject ourselves or sabotage our happiness, freedom, and love.

From now on, let every action, every reaction, every thought, every emotion, be based on love. Help us Creator, to increase our self-love until the entire dream of our life is transformed, from fear and drama to love and joy. Let the power of our self-love be strong enough to break all the lies we were programmed to believe- all the lies that tell us we are not good enough, or strong enough, or intelligent enough, that we cannot make it. Let the power of our self-love be so strong that we no longer need to live our life according to other people's opinions. Let us trust ourselves completely to make the choices we must make. With our self-love, we are no longer afraid to face any responsibility in our life or face any problems and resolve them as they arise. Whatever we want to accomplish, let it be done with the power of our self-love.

Starting today, help us to love ourselves so much that we never set up any circumstances that go against us. We can live our life being ourselves and not pretending to be someone else just to be accepted by other people. We no longer need other people to accept us or tell us how good we are because we know what we are. With the power of our self-love, let us enjoy what we see every time we look in the mirror. Let there be a big smile on our face that embraces our inner and outer beauty. Help us to feel such intense self-love that we always enjoy our own presence.

Let us love ourselves without judgment, because when we judge, we carry blame and guilt, we have the need for punishment, and we lose the perspective of your love. Strengthen our will to forgive ourselves at this moment. Clean our minds of emotional, poison and self-judgments so we can live in complete peace and love.

Let our self love be the power that changes the dream of our life. With this new power in our hearts, the power of self-love, let us transform every relationship we have, being with the relationship we have with ourselves. Help us to be free of any conflict with others. Help us be happy to share our time with our loved ones and to forgive them for any injustice we feel in our mind. Help us to love ourselves so much that we forgive anyone who ever hurt us in our life.

Give us the courage to love our family and friends unconditionally, and to change our relationships in the most positive and loving way. Help us to create new channels of communication in our relationships, so there is no war of control, there is no winner or loser. Together let us work as a team for love, for joy, for harmony.

Let our relationship with our family and friends be based on respect and joy, so we no longer have the need to tell them how to think or how to be. Let our romantic relationship be the most wonderful relationship; let us feel joy every time we share ourselves with our partner. Help us to accept others just the way they are, without judgment, because when we reject them, we reject ourselves. When we reject ourselves, we reject you.

Today is a new beginning. Help us to start our life over beginning today with the power of self-love. Help us to enjoy our life, to enjoy our relationships, to explore life, to take risks, to be alive, and to no longer live in fear of love. Let us open our hearts to the love that is our birthright. Help us to become masters of gratitude, generosity, and love so that we can enjoy all of your creation forever and ever. Amen."

Acknowledgments

This book has been dormant inside of me for over a decade. When the timing is right, God has a way of creating the space and understanding for life to be breathed into and to propel us into our next season. Then God aligns us with the right people and opportunities in order to bring it all to fruition. This book is the product of such a divine encounter, and I would be remiss if I didn't take this opportunity to thank a few people as it would not have been possible without some angelic intervention.

One week before my aha moment in Nashville, I was having a coaching session with Dr. Loren Michaels Harris. He is not only my coach, but he's also my mentor and friend. I had been working with him for about nine months, and I credit him for helping me to gain the confidence and connection to my God-given talents and to my deepest goals and aspirations in order to step into this next season of Speaking, Coaching, and writing my book. During that session, he abruptly changed topics from what we were speaking about and said, "I remember you said you started writing a book many years ago. When are you going to finish it?" I gave him a litany of excuses, and he looked straight at me and gave me the Dr. Loren 'Cut the Bullshit' look and I said, "OK, I am out of excuses! It is time!" The seed was planted. It was then watered in Nashville by the UnleashU family and Dr. Obom Bowen.

During the execution phase, my family and friends have been amazing and supportive and have called, texted and stopped by to check on me to make sure I was eating and taking care of myself. I am truly grateful. Dr. Loren has continued to be pivotal in guiding me through this process with grace, compassion (especially when I had an ugly cry) and he encouraged me to get uncomfortable in order to make decisions that are truly in alignment with what I am trying to create.

He also delivered several divine messages to me in a way that only he can. His ability to be the conduit of divine accordance is truly a gift. His leadership and intuition guided and helped me tap into a piece of myself that I didn't know existed. In that sacred space, I was able to see exactly what I wanted the cover of this book to look like and how to express that to the publisher. I am indebted and so grateful for his giftings, guidance, support, honesty and integrity.

Michael Fabber and the UnleashU Family have been incredible cheerleaders and have offered me a wealth of knowledge about the best ways to launch my book, coaching program and business as a whole. Social Media and Marketing are not my forte, so I am grateful Michael loves it so much that he has the patience to teach me in a way that I can understand and make actionable.

I am grateful to Lynda Sunshine West and Sally Larkin Green with Action Takers Publishing for editing and publishing this book. They made this process easy and enjoyable, and from the moment they connected with the project they were all in! It's been a joy to work with them, and they are as excited as I am to see this book come to life!

I am incredibly thankful God saw fit to align me with all these selfless individuals who have advised, inspired, supported and motivated me more than they will ever know. They have also taken my hand and offered their resources and platforms to ensure this project is successful. My heart is so full, and I just wanted to say a huge thank you! It's GO Season!

With Gratitude,
Martha Glory Stecker Kartaoui

READER BONUS!

Dear Reader,

As a thank you for your support, I would like to offer you a special reader bonus: The 40-Day Woosah Gratitude Journal.

The Journal typically retails for $14.95, but as a valued reader, you can access the PDF version for free. To claim your free download, click on the QR code.

Kids Woosah Journal   **Adults Woosah Journal**

With Gratitude,
Martha

READER BONUS!

Made in the USA
Monee, IL
07 November 2024